While every precaution has been taken in the prej
publisher assumes no responsibility for errors or c
resulting from the use of the information contain

WHEAT-FREE COOKING GUIDE: LIVING A HEALTHIER LIFE
WITH WHEAT-FREE

First edition. March 21, 2024.

Copyright © 2024 Brintalos Georgios.

ISBN: 979-8224318179

Written by Brintalos Georgios.

Table of Contents

Wheat-Free Cooking Guide: Living A Healthier Life With Wheat-Free

Quinoa stuffed peppers

Ingredients:
- 4 bell peppers
- 1 cup quinoa
- 1 1/2 cups vegetable broth
- 1 can black beans
- 1 cup corn
- 1 tsp cumin
- 1/2 tsp chili powder
- 1/2 cup shredded cheese

Equipment:
1. Knife
2. Cutting board
3. Skillet
4. Mixing bowl
5. Spoon

Methods:
Step 1: Preheat the oven to 375°F.

Step 2: Cut the tops off of 4 large bell peppers and remove the seeds and membranes.

Step 3: In a large bowl, mix together 1 cup cooked quinoa, 1 can of black beans (drained and rinsed), 1 cup diced tomatoes, 1/2 cup corn kernels, 1/2 cup diced red onion, 1 tsp cumin, 1 tsp chili powder, and salt and pepper to taste.

Step 4: Stuff the quinoa mixture into the peppers and place them in a baking dish.

Step 5: Cover the dish with foil and bake for 25-30 minutes, until the peppers are tender.

Step 6: Serve hot and enjoy!

Helpful Tips:
1. Precook the quinoa before stuffing the peppers to ensure it's fully cooked.

2. Use a flavorful broth to cook the quinoa for added taste.

3. Chop vegetables finely for even distribution throughout the stuffing mixture.

4. Add herbs and spices to the quinoa mixture for extra flavor.

5. Consider using a mix of different colored bell peppers for visual appeal.

6. Top stuffed peppers with cheese for a delicious finishing touch.

7. Bake the stuffed peppers covered in foil to keep them moist, then uncover for the last 10 minutes to brown the cheese.

8. Enjoy quinoa stuffed peppers as a healthy and satisfying meal or side dish.

Cabbage roll bowls

Ingredients:
- 1 head of cabbage
- 1 lb ground beef
- 1 onion, chopped
- 1 cup cooked rice
- 1 can diced tomatoes
- 1 tbsp tomato paste
- 1 tsp garlic powder
- 1 tsp paprika
- Salt and pepper to taste

Equipment:
1. Pot
2. Pan
3. Knife
4. Cutting board
5. Mixing bowl
6. Tongs

Methods:
Step 1: Preheat the oven to 375°F.

Step 2: Remove the core from a head of cabbage and blanch the leaves in boiling water for 2-3 minutes.

Step 3: In a large bowl, mix together ground beef, cooked rice, onions, garlic, and seasonings.

Step 4: Place a scoop of the meat mixture onto each cabbage leaf and roll them up like a burrito.

Step 5: Place the cabbage rolls in a baking dish and top with marinara sauce.

Step 6: Cover the dish with foil and bake for 45 minutes.

Step 7: Serve hot and enjoy your delicious cabbage roll bowls.

Helpful Tips:

BRINTALOS GEORGIOS

1. Choose a cabbage head that is large and has tightly packed leaves for easy rolling.

2. Carefully remove the core of the cabbage head to make separating the leaves easier.

3. Blanch the cabbage leaves in boiling water for a few minutes to soften them before rolling.

4. Stuff the cabbage leaves with a flavorful mixture of meat, rice, and seasonings.

5. Use kitchen twine to secure the cabbage rolls so they hold their shape while cooking.

6. Cook the cabbage rolls in a flavorful tomato-based sauce to enhance the flavors.

7. Serve the cabbage roll bowls with a side of sour cream or yogurt for added richness.

Beef and snap pea stir-fry

Ingredients:
- 1 lb beef sliced thinly
- 2 cups snap peas
- 1 onion sliced
- 2 cloves garlic minced
- 1/4 cup soy sauce
- 1 tbsp sesame oil

Equipment:
1. Wok
2. Spatula
3. Knife
4. Cutting board
5. Tongs

Methods:
Step 1: Heat 1 tablespoon of oil in a large skillet over high heat.

Step 2: Add 1 pound of thinly sliced beef and cook until browned, about 3-4 minutes.

Step 3: Remove beef from skillet and set aside.

Step 4: In the same skillet, add 1 tablespoon of oil and stir in 2 cups of snap peas.

Step 5: Cook the snap peas until they are bright green and slightly tender, about 2-3 minutes.

Step 6: Add the beef back into the skillet and stir to combine.

Step 7: Pour in 1/4 cup of soy sauce and 1 tablespoon of oyster sauce, stirring until heated through.

Step 8: Serve the beef and snap pea stir-fry over rice and enjoy!

Helpful Tips:
1. Start by slicing your beef thinly against the grain to ensure tenderness.

2. Marinate the beef in a mixture of soy sauce, ginger, and garlic for at least 30 minutes for maximum flavor.

3. Use a wok or large skillet to quickly stir-fry the beef over high heat to lock in juices and prevent toughness.

4. Add snap peas towards the end of cooking to retain their crunch and vibrant color.

5. Finish with a splash of sesame oil and a sprinkle of sesame seeds for added depth of flavor. Enjoy your delicious and nutritious beef and snap pea stir-fry!

Cauliflower fried rice with chicken

Ingredients:
- 1 head cauliflower, grated
- 2 chicken breasts, diced
- 1 onion, chopped
- 2 eggs
- Soy sauce, to taste
- Garlic powder, to taste
- Sesame oil, for cooking

Equipment:
1. Frying pan
2. Spatula
3. Knife
4. Cutting board
5. Mixing bowl

Methods:
Step 1: Cut 1 head of cauliflower into florets and pulse in a food processor until rice-like consistency.

Step 2: Cook 2 chicken breasts in a skillet with oil until fully cooked. Remove and set aside.

Step 3: In the same skillet, cook 1 diced onion, 2 minced garlic cloves, 1 diced carrot, and 1 diced bell pepper until softened.

Step 4: Add the riced cauliflower to the skillet and cook until slightly browned.

Step 5: Stir in 2 beaten eggs and cooked chicken, breaking up the eggs as they cook.

Step 6: Season with soy sauce, sesame oil, and pepper.

Step 7: Enjoy your cauliflower fried rice with chicken!

Helpful Tips:
1. Start by cutting the cauliflower into small florets and pulse in a food processor until it resembles rice.

2. Cook the chicken in a separate pan before adding it to the cauliflower rice to ensure it's fully cooked.

3. Add plenty of vegetables like bell peppers, peas, and carrots for added texture and flavor.

4. Season with soy sauce, garlic, ginger, and a pinch of red pepper flakes for an extra kick.

5. Make sure to constantly stir the cauliflower rice to prevent it from sticking to the pan.

6. Top with chopped green onions and a drizzle of sesame oil before serving. Enjoy!

Chicken lettuce wraps with peanut sauce

Ingredients:
- 1 lb chicken breast (diced)
- 1 onion (chopped)
- 2 cloves garlic (minced)
- 1/4 cup soy sauce
- 1/4 cup peanut butter
- 1 tbsp honey
- 1 head lettuce (sliced)
- 1/4 cup peanuts (chopped)

Equipment:
1. Wok
2. Mixing bowls
3. Wooden spoon
4. Knife
5. Cutting board

Methods:
Step 1: Heat oil in a large skillet over medium heat.

Step 2: Add diced chicken and cook until no longer pink.

Step 3: Stir in minced garlic, ginger, and diced red bell pepper.

Step 4: In a small bowl, mix together soy sauce, hoisin sauce, and peanut butter for the sauce.

Step 5: Pour the sauce over the chicken mixture in the skillet and stir to combine.

Step 6: Arrange lettuce leaves on a platter and spoon the chicken mixture into each leaf.

Step 7: Garnish with chopped peanuts and cilantro before serving.

Step 8: Enjoy your delicious chicken lettuce wraps with peanut sauce!

Helpful Tips:
1. Start by marinating the chicken in soy sauce, ginger, and garlic for at least 30 minutes before cooking.

2. Cook the chicken in a hot skillet with a little bit of oil until it is cooked through and slightly browned.

3. Mix together peanut butter, soy sauce, lime juice, honey, and a dash of sesame oil to create the perfect peanut sauce.

4. Wash and separate the lettuce leaves to use as the wraps.

5. Fill each lettuce leaf with the cooked chicken and top with the peanut sauce.

6. Serve your chicken lettuce wraps with a side of rice or quinoa for a complete meal. Enjoy!

Spicy shrimp and zucchini noodles

Ingredients:
- 1 lb shrimp
- 2 large zucchinis
- 2 tbsp olive oil
- 1 tsp red pepper flakes
- Salt and pepper to taste

Equipment:
1. Skillet
2. Spiralizer
3. Tongs
4. Mixing bowl
5. Chef's knife

Methods:
Step 1: Heat a large skillet over medium heat and add olive oil.

Step 2: Add chopped garlic and red pepper flakes to the skillet and cook for 1-2 minutes.

Step 3: Add peeled and deveined shrimp to the skillet and cook until they turn pink, about 3-4 minutes.

Step 4: Remove the shrimp from the skillet and set aside.

Step 5: Add spiralized zucchini noodles to the skillet and cook for 2-3 minutes.

Step 6: Return the shrimp to the skillet and toss with the zucchini noodles.

Step 7: Season with salt, pepper, and a squeeze of lemon juice.

Step 8: Serve hot and enjoy!

Helpful Tips:
1. Marinate the shrimp in a spicy marinade for at least 30 minutes to infuse flavor.

2. Use large shrimp for more meatiness and flavor.

3. Spiralize the zucchini noodles for a healthier alternative to traditional pasta noodles.

4. Cook the zucchini noodles just until tender to avoid them becoming mushy.

5. Add extra heat with red pepper flakes or chopped jalapeños.

6. Garnish with fresh herbs like cilantro or parsley for a burst of freshness.

7. Serve with a squeeze of lime to balance the spiciness.

Roasted salmon with lemon dill sauce

Ingredients:
- 4 salmon fillets
- 1 lemon
- 2 tablespoons fresh dill
- 2 tablespoons olive oil
- Salt and pepper to taste

Equipment:
1. Baking sheet
2. Saucepan
3. Whisk
4. Tongs
5. Wooden spoon

Methods:
Step 1: Preheat the oven to 425 degrees F.

Step 2: Place a salmon fillet on a baking sheet lined with parchment paper.

Step 3: Drizzle the salmon with olive oil and season with salt and pepper.

Step 4: Roast the salmon in the oven for 12-15 minutes, or until cooked through.

Step 5: While the salmon is cooking, make the lemon dill sauce by combining mayonnaise, lemon juice, dill, salt, and pepper in a small bowl.

Step 6: Serve the roasted salmon with the lemon dill sauce drizzled on top.

Step 7: Enjoy your delicious roasted salmon with lemon dill sauce!

Helpful Tips:
1. Preheat your oven to 400°F and line a baking sheet with parchment paper.

2. Place the salmon fillets on the baking sheet and season with salt, pepper, and a drizzle of olive oil.

3. Roast the salmon in the oven for 12-15 minutes, or until the fillets are cooked through and flake easily with a fork.

4. While the salmon is roasting, prepare the lemon dill sauce by combining mayo, lemon juice, fresh dill, salt, and pepper in a bowl.

5. Serve the roasted salmon topped with the lemon dill sauce and garnish with additional fresh dill. Enjoy!

Greek chicken and vegetable skewers

Ingredients:

- 1 lb boneless, skinless chicken breast
- 1 red onion, cut into chunks
- 1 red bell pepper, cut into chunks
- 1 zucchini, sliced
- 1/4 cup olive oil
- 2 cloves garlic, minced
- 1 tsp dried oregano
- Salt and pepper to taste

Equipment:

1. Skewers
2. Grill
3. Tongs
4. Basting brush
5. Cutting board

Methods:

Step 1: Preheat the grill to medium-high heat.

Step 2: In a bowl, mix olive oil, lemon juice, garlic, oregano, salt, and pepper.

Step 3: Cut chicken and vegetables into bite-sized pieces.

Step 4: Marinate the chicken and vegetables in the olive oil mixture for at least 30 minutes.

Step 5: Thread chicken and vegetables onto skewers, alternating between chicken and vegetables.

Step 6: Place skewers on the grill and cook for 10-15 minutes, turning occasionally, until chicken is cooked through and vegetables are tender.

Step 7: Serve the skewers hot with a side of tzatziki sauce or a Greek salad. Enjoy!

Helpful Tips:

BRINTALOS GEORGIOS

1. Marinate the chicken in a mixture of Greek yogurt, lemon juice, olive oil, garlic, and herbs for at least 30 minutes before skewering.

2. Use a variety of colorful vegetables like bell peppers, cherry tomatoes, red onion, and zucchini for a visually appealing presentation.

3. Soak wooden skewers in water for at least 30 minutes to prevent them from burning on the grill.

4. Preheat the grill to medium-high heat and brush with oil to prevent sticking.

5. Rotate the skewers regularly on the grill to ensure even cooking of both the chicken and vegetables.

6. Serve with a side of tzatziki sauce for dipping and enjoy!

Cauliflower crust pizza with veggies

Ingredients:
- 1 head cauliflower
- 1/2 cup shredded mozzarella
- 1/4 cup grated Parmesan
- 1/2 tsp dried oregano
- 1/2 tsp garlic powder
- 1/4 tsp salt
- 1 egg
- 1/2 cup marinara sauce
- Assorted veggies of choice

Equipment:
1. Knife
2. Cutting board
3. Baking sheet
4. Mixing bowl
5. Vegetable peeler
6. Pizza cutter

Methods:
Step 1: Preheat the oven to 400°F and line a baking sheet with parchment paper.

Step 2: Break a head of cauliflower into florets and pulse in a food processor until finely chopped.

Step 3: Microwave the cauliflower for 5 minutes, then let it cool.

Step 4: Squeeze out any excess moisture from the cauliflower using a kitchen towel.

Step 5: Mix the cauliflower with 1 egg, 1/2 cup shredded mozzarella cheese, and seasonings.

Step 6: Spread the cauliflower mixture onto the prepared baking sheet and form a pizza crust.

Step 7: Bake the crust for 25 minutes, then top with desired veggies and cheese.

Step 8: Bake for an additional 10 minutes or until the cheese is melted and bubbly. Enjoy your cauliflower crust pizza with veggies!

Helpful Tips:

1. Precook cauliflower rice and squeeze out excess moisture to ensure a crispy crust.

2. Blend cauliflower rice with 1 egg, 1/2 cup shredded mozzarella, garlic powder, and Italian seasoning to make the crust.

3. Bake the crust first for 20 minutes at 400°F before adding toppings.

4. Use a variety of colorful veggies like bell peppers, onions, mushrooms, and tomatoes for a tasty topping.

5. Precook veggies slightly to ensure they are cooked through when the pizza is done.

6. Top with a light layer of tomato sauce and sprinkle with more cheese before baking for an additional 10-15 minutes. Enjoy your delicious homemade cauliflower crust pizza with veggies!

Baked chicken thighs with rosemary

Ingredients:
- 8 chicken thighs
- 1 tbsp olive oil
- 2 cloves garlic, minced
- 2 tsp fresh rosemary, chopped
- Salt and pepper to taste

Equipment:
1. Baking dish
2. Tongs
3. Knife
4. Cutting board
5. Oven
6. Cooking thermometer

Methods:
Step 1: Preheat the oven to 400°F and line a baking sheet with aluminum foil.

Step 2: Pat dry the chicken thighs with paper towels and place them on the baking sheet.

Step 3: Drizzle olive oil over the chicken thighs and season with salt, pepper, and dried rosemary.

Step 4: Rub the seasonings into the chicken thighs until they are evenly coated.

Step 5: Bake in the preheated oven for 35-40 minutes or until the chicken is cooked through and the skin is crispy.

Step 6: Let the chicken thighs rest for 5 minutes before serving. Enjoy your baked chicken thighs with rosemary!

Helpful Tips:
1. Preheat your oven to 400°F.
2. Rub the chicken thighs with olive oil, salt, pepper, and minced rosemary.
3. Place the chicken thighs on a baking sheet lined with parchment paper.

4. Bake for 25-30 minutes or until the internal temperature reaches 165°F.

5. For extra flavor, consider adding lemon slices or garlic cloves to the baking dish.

6. Let the chicken thighs rest for 5 minutes before serving.

7. Serve the baked chicken thighs with your favorite side dishes like roasted vegetables or mashed potatoes. Enjoy your delicious meal!

Eggplant parmesan with ground turkey

Ingredients:
- 1 large eggplant
- 1 lb ground turkey
- 1 cup marinara sauce
- 1/2 cup shredded mozzarella cheese
- 1/4 cup grated parmesan cheese
- 1/4 cup breadcrumbs

Equipment:
1. Skillet
2. Baking dish
3. Mixing bowl
4. Knife
5. Grater

Methods:
Step 1: Preheat the oven to 375°F.

Step 2: Slice the eggplant into 1/4 inch rounds.

Step 3: Heat olive oil in a skillet and cook ground turkey until browned.

Step 4: Add marinara sauce to the skillet and let simmer.

Step 5: In a separate bowl, beat eggs and dip eggplant slices in the egg mixture.

Step 6: Coat the eggplant slices in breadcrumbs.

Step 7: Heat olive oil in a separate skillet and fry the eggplant slices until golden brown.

Step 8: In a baking dish, layer the fried eggplant, ground turkey mixture, and shredded mozzarella cheese.

Step 9: Repeat the layers and bake in the oven for 25-30 minutes.

Step 10: Let cool before serving. Enjoy your delicious eggplant parmesan with ground turkey!

Helpful Tips:
1. Start by preheating your oven to 375°F.

BRINTALOS GEORGIOS

2. Slice the eggplant into 1/4 inch rounds and sprinkle with salt to draw out any bitterness.

3. Brown the ground turkey in a skillet with olive oil, minced garlic, and Italian seasoning.

4. Layer the eggplant, ground turkey, marinara sauce, and shredded mozzarella in a baking dish.

5. Repeat the layers until all ingredients are used, ending with a layer of cheese on top.

6. Cover the dish with foil and bake for 45 minutes, then remove the foil and bake for an additional 15 minutes until bubbly and golden brown.

7. Let it cool for a few minutes before serving. Enjoy!

Broiled tilapia with mango salsa

Ingredients:
- 4 tilapia fillets
- 2 ripe mangoes
- 1 red bell pepper
- 1/2 red onion
- Fresh cilantro
- Lime juice
- Olive oil
- Salt and pepper

Equipment:
1. Knife
2. Cutting board
3. Skillet
4. Mixing bowl
5. Spatula

Methods:
Step 1: Preheat the broiler and line a baking sheet with foil.

Step 2: Season the tilapia fillets with salt, pepper, and olive oil.

Step 3: Place the seasoned fillets on the prepared baking sheet.

Step 4: Broil the tilapia for 6-8 minutes until it flakes easily with a fork.

Step 5: While the tilapia is cooking, prepare the mango salsa by combining diced mango, red onion, jalapeno, cilantro, lime juice, and salt.

Step 6: Serve the broiled tilapia topped with mango salsa.

Step 7: Enjoy your delicious and healthy meal!

Helpful Tips:
1. Preheat the broiler and season the tilapia with salt, pepper, and a squeeze of lemon juice.

2. Make the mango salsa by combining diced mango, red onion, jalapeno, cilantro, and lime juice in a bowl.

3. Place the tilapia on a broiler pan and broil for 5-7 minutes per side, until the fish is cooked through and flakes easily with a fork.

4. Top the broiled tilapia with the mango salsa before serving for a fresh and flavorful contrast.

5. Serve the dish with a side of rice or quinoa for a complete and balanced meal. Enjoy!

Chicken and vegetable sheet pan dinner

Ingredients:
- 4 chicken breasts
- 2 bell peppers
- 2 zucchinis
- 1 red onion
- 2 tbsp olive oil
- 1 tsp garlic powder
- Salt and pepper to taste

Equipment:
1. Baking sheet
2. Mixing bowl
3. Whisk
4. Knife
5. Cutting board

Methods:
Step 1: Preheat the oven to 400°F.

Step 2: Season boneless, skinless chicken breasts with salt, pepper, and your choice of herbs.

Step 3: Chop assorted vegetables such as bell peppers, zucchini, and red onion.

Step 4: Toss the vegetables with olive oil, salt, and pepper.

Step 5: Place the chicken breasts on a baking sheet and surround them with the vegetables.

Step 6: Roast in the oven for 25-30 minutes, or until the chicken is cooked through and the vegetables are tender.

Step 7: Serve hot and enjoy your delicious chicken and vegetable sheet pan dinner!

Helpful Tips:
1. Preheat your oven to 400°F.
2. Season the chicken and vegetables with your favorite herbs and spices.

3. Cut the chicken and vegetables into similar sized pieces for even cooking.

4. Use a rimmed baking sheet lined with parchment paper to prevent sticking.

5. Arrange the chicken and vegetables in a single layer on the baking sheet to ensure they cook evenly.

6. Drizzle with olive oil and toss everything together to coat evenly.

7. Roast in the preheated oven for 25-30 minutes, or until the chicken is cooked through and the vegetables are tender.

8. Serve hot and enjoy a delicious and easy meal!

Grilled pork chops with apple chutney

Ingredients:
- 4 pork chops
- 2 apples, diced
- 1/4 cup brown sugar
- 1/4 cup apple cider vinegar
- 1/2 tsp cinnamon
- Salt and pepper to taste

Equipment:
1. Grill pan
2. Tongs
3. Chef's knife
4. Cutting board
5. Saucepan
6. Wooden spoon

Methods:
Step 1: Preheat the grill to medium-high heat.

Step 2: Season pork chops with salt, pepper, and your favorite spices.

Step 3: Grill pork chops for 4-5 minutes on each side, or until they reach an internal temperature of 145°F.

Step 4: Remove pork chops from the grill and let them rest for a few minutes.

Step 5: In a saucepan, combine diced apples, brown sugar, apple cider vinegar, and spices to make the chutney.

Step 6: Cook the chutney over medium heat until the apples are tender and the mixture thickens.

Step 7: Serve the grilled pork chops with the apple chutney on top. Enjoy!

Helpful Tips:
1. Start by marinating the pork chops in a mixture of olive oil, salt, pepper, and any desired herbs for at least 30 minutes.

2. Preheat your grill to medium-high heat and oil the grates to prevent sticking.

3. Grill the pork chops for about 4-5 minutes on each side, or until they reach an internal temperature of 145°F.

4. While the pork chops are grilling, prepare the apple chutney by sautéing diced apples, onions, brown sugar, vinegar, and spices in a pan until soft and fragrant.

5. Serve the grilled pork chops with a generous spoonful of apple chutney on top for a delicious and flavorful meal.

Turkey and avocado roll-ups

Ingredients:

- 8 slices of turkey
- 1 avocado
- 1/4 cup of cream cheese
- 1/4 cup of diced tomatoes
- Salt and pepper to taste

Equipment:

1. Knife
2. Cutting board
3. Skillet
4. Spatula
5. Mixing bowl

Methods:

Step 1: Lay out one large tortilla on a flat surface.

Step 2: Spread a layer of mashed avocado evenly over the tortilla.

Step 3: Place slices of roasted turkey on top of the avocado.

Step 4: Sprinkle shredded cheese over the turkey.

Step 5: Roll up the tortilla tightly to create a wrap.

Step 6: Use a sharp knife to slice the wrap into smaller roll-ups.

Step 7: Serve the turkey and avocado roll-ups as a delicious and easy snack or lunch option. Enjoy!

Helpful Tips:

1. Start by preparing your ingredients: thinly slice turkey breast and avocado, and gather some lettuce leaves.

2. Lay out a slice of turkey on a cutting board, add a layer of avocado and lettuce on top.

3. Roll up the turkey, avocado, and lettuce tightly to create a compact roll-up.

4. Secure the roll-up with toothpicks to hold everything together.

5. Serve the Turkey and avocado roll-ups as a light and healthy snack or meal option. Enjoy!

6. You can also add other ingredients such as cheese, tomato, or cucumber for added flavor and texture.

Roasted cauliflower steaks

Ingredients:
- 1 large head of cauliflower
- 2 tbsp olive oil
- 1 tsp garlic powder
- 1 tsp paprika
- Salt and pepper, to taste

Equipment:
1. Knife
2. Cutting board
3. Baking sheet
4. Tongs
5. Oven
6. Plate

Methods:
Step 1: Preheat the oven to 400°F.

Step 2: Remove the leaves from a head of cauliflower and trim the stem end.

Step 3: Cut the cauliflower into 1-inch thick slices to make steaks.

Step 4: Place the cauliflower steaks on a baking sheet lined with parchment paper.

Step 5: Drizzle olive oil over the cauliflower steaks and season with salt, pepper, and your favorite herbs or spices.

Step 6: Roast in the preheated oven for 30-40 minutes, flipping halfway through, until the cauliflower is golden brown and tender.

Step 7: Serve the roasted cauliflower steaks hot as a delicious and healthy meatless meal.

Helpful Tips:
1. Preheat your oven to 425°F to ensure a crispy outside while keeping the inside tender.

2. Cut cauliflower into 1-inch thick slices to create "steaks" for even cooking.

BRINTALOS GEORGIOS

3. Brush both sides of cauliflower steaks with olive oil and season with salt, pepper, and any desired herbs or spices.

4. Place cauliflower steaks on a baking sheet lined with parchment paper or a silicone mat to prevent sticking.

5. Roast cauliflower steaks for 20-25 minutes, flipping halfway through, until golden brown and fork-tender.

6. Serve with a squeeze of fresh lemon juice or a drizzle of balsamic glaze for added flavor.

Beef and broccoli stir-fry

Ingredients:
- 1 lb beef strips
- 3 cups broccoli florets
- 1/4 cup soy sauce
- 2 tbsp sesame oil
- 2 cloves garlic
- 1 tsp ginger
- 1 tbsp cornstarch

Equipment:
1. Wok
2. Spatula
3. Tongs
4. Cutting board
5. Knife

Methods:
Step 1: Slice 1 lb of beef into thin strips and marinate with soy sauce, garlic, and ginger for at least 30 minutes.

Step 2: In a hot pan or wok, stir-fry the marinated beef in vegetable oil until browned. Remove from pan and set aside.

Step 3: Stir-fry 2 cups of broccoli florets and sliced bell peppers in the same pan until slightly tender.

Step 4: Add the beef back into the pan and pour in a mixture of soy sauce, oyster sauce, and brown sugar. Cook until heated through and sauce has thickened.

Step 5: Serve hot over steamed rice. Enjoy your beef and broccoli stir-fry!

Helpful Tips:
1. Start by slicing the beef thinly against the grain to ensure tenderness.

2. Marinate the beef in a mixture of soy sauce, garlic, and ginger for at least 30 minutes for maximum flavor.

3. Use a wok or large skillet for even cooking and quick stir-frying.

4. Cook the beef first until browned, then remove from the pan before cooking the broccoli to avoid overcooking.

5. Add the beef back to the pan along with the broccoli and sauce to finish cooking together.

6. Serve over steamed rice for a complete and delicious meal.

Shrimp and vegetable stir-fried rice

Ingredients:
- 1 lb shrimp
- 2 cups mixed vegetables
- 3 cups cooked rice
- 4 tbsp soy sauce

Equipment:
1. Wok
2. Wooden spatula
3. Chef's knife
4. Cutting board
5. Rice cooker
6. Strainer

Methods:
Step 1: Cook 1 cup of rice according to package instructions and set aside.

Step 2: Heat 1 tablespoon of oil in a large skillet over medium-high heat.

Step 3: Add 1 pound of shrimp and cook until pink, about 2-3 minutes per side. Remove from skillet and set aside.

Step 4: In the same skillet, add 1 tablespoon of oil and stir-fry 2 cups of mixed vegetables (such as bell peppers, carrots, and peas) for 3-4 minutes.

Step 5: Add the cooked rice and shrimp back to the skillet and stir to combine.

Step 6: Season with soy sauce, salt, and pepper to taste.

Step 7: Serve hot and enjoy your delicious shrimp and vegetable stir-fried rice!

Helpful Tips:
1. Start by cooking the rice first and letting it cool down before using it in the stir-fry.

2. Cut all your vegetables and shrimp into bite-sized pieces to ensure even cooking.

3. Use a high heat and preheat your wok or large skillet before adding any ingredients.

4. Cook the shrimp first until they are pink and opaque, then remove them from the pan.

5. Add your vegetables next, starting with the ones that take the longest to cook.

6. Season with soy sauce, oyster sauce, and any other seasonings you prefer.

7. Add the cooked shrimp back in and stir everything together before serving hot.

Turkey and vegetable skillet

Ingredients:
- 1 lb ground turkey
- 1 bell pepper, diced
- 1 zucchini, sliced
- 1 onion, chopped
- 2 cloves garlic, minced
- 1 tsp olive oil
- Salt and pepper to taste

Equipment:
1. Skillet
2. Chef's knife
3. Cutting board
4. Wooden spoon
5. Tongs

Methods:
Step 1: Heat a large skillet over medium heat and add olive oil.

Step 2: Sauté diced onions and minced garlic until softened.

Step 3: Add diced turkey breast to the skillet and cook until browned.

Step 4: Season with salt, pepper, and your favorite herbs and spices.

Step 5: Add sliced bell peppers, zucchini, and cherry tomatoes to the skillet.

Step 6: Cook until vegetables are tender but still slightly crisp.

Step 7: Serve the turkey and vegetable skillet hot, garnished with fresh herbs.

Step 8: Enjoy your delicious and healthy meal!

Helpful Tips:
1. Start by heating a skillet over medium-high heat and add cooking oil.

2. Season your turkey breast with salt, pepper, and your favorite herbs or spices before cooking.

3. Cook the turkey on one side until browned, then flip and cook the other side until fully cooked through.

4. Remove the turkey from the skillet and set aside.

5. Add sliced vegetables like bell peppers, onions, and zucchini to the skillet and stir-fry until tender-crisp.

6. Season the vegetables with salt, pepper, and additional herbs or spices to taste.

7. Serve the cooked turkey slices on top of the vegetable mixture for a tasty and healthy meal.

Grilled chicken and vegetable salad

Ingredients:
- 2 chicken breasts
- 2 bell peppers
- 1 zucchini
- 1 red onion
- 1/4 cup olive oil
- Salt and pepper to taste

Equipment:
1. Grill pan
2. Tongs
3. Mixing bowl
4. Chef's knife
5. Cutting board

Methods:
Step 1: Marinate chicken breasts in a mixture of olive oil, lemon juice, garlic, salt, and pepper for at least 30 minutes.

Step 2: Preheat the grill to medium-high heat.

Step 3: Grill chicken breasts for 6-8 minutes on each side, or until fully cooked.

Step 4: While the chicken is cooking, chop your favorite vegetables such as bell peppers, zucchini, and cherry tomatoes.

Step 5: Toss the vegetables in olive oil, salt, and pepper.

Step 6: Grill the vegetables for 3-4 minutes on each side, or until they are slightly charred.

Step 7: Slice the grilled chicken breasts and serve over the grilled vegetables. Enjoy your delicious grilled chicken and vegetable salad!

Helpful Tips:
1. Marinate chicken in a mixture of olive oil, lemon juice, garlic, and herbs for at least an hour before grilling.

2. Preheat the grill to medium-high heat before adding the chicken.

3. Grill the chicken for about 6-8 minutes per side or until internal temperature reaches 165°F.

4. Toss chopped vegetables (like bell peppers, zucchini, and cherry tomatoes) in olive oil and seasonings before grilling in a grill basket.

5. Cook vegetables for about 5-7 minutes or until they are tender-crisp.

6. Combine grilled chicken and vegetables with a mix of baby greens, avocado, and a light vinaigrette for a delicious salad.

Beef and zucchini noodles stir-fry

Ingredients:
- 1 lb of beef strips
- 2 zucchinis, spiralized
- 1/4 cup of soy sauce
- 2 cloves of garlic
- 1 tbsp of ginger
- 1 tsp of sesame oil
- 1/2 tsp of red pepper flakes
- 1 tbsp of olive oil
- Salt and pepper to taste

Equipment:
1. Wok
2. Spatula
3. Knife
4. Cutting board
5. Cooking oil
6. Seasonings

Methods:
Step 1: Slice one pound of sirloin beef into thin strips.

Step 2: Heat two tablespoons of oil in a large pan over medium-high heat.

Step 3: Add the beef strips to the pan and cook until browned, about 3-4 minutes.

Step 4: Remove the beef from the pan and set aside.

Step 5: In the same pan, add two sliced zucchinis and cook for 2-3 minutes until slightly softened.

Step 6: Add the beef back to the pan with the zucchini.

Step 7: Pour in a mixture of soy sauce, garlic, and ginger.

Step 8: Cook for an additional 2-3 minutes, stirring occasionally.

Step 9: Serve the stir-fry over zucchini noodles and enjoy!

Helpful Tips:

BRINTALOS GEORGIOS

1. Start by marinating thinly sliced beef in a mixture of soy sauce, garlic, and ginger for at least 30 minutes.

2. Use a spiralizer to create zucchini noodles as a healthy alternative to traditional noodles.

3. Stir-fry the marinated beef in a hot pan until browned and cooked through.

4. Remove the beef from the pan and stir-fry the zucchini noodles until slightly softened.

5. Add the beef back to the pan along with any desired vegetables, such as bell peppers or mushrooms.

6. Season with soy sauce, sesame oil, and a pinch of red pepper flakes for added flavor.

7. Serve hot and enjoy your delicious beef and zucchini noodles stir-fry.

Turkey and kale stuffed portobello mushrooms

Ingredients:
- 4 large portobello mushrooms
- 1 lb ground turkey
- 2 cups chopped kale
- 1/2 cup grated Parmesan cheese
- 2 cloves minced garlic
- Salt and pepper to taste

Equipment:
1. Knife
2. Cutting board
3. Mixing bowl
4. Baking sheet
5. Spoon
6. Skillet

Methods:
Step 1: Preheat the oven to 375°F and prepare a baking sheet with parchment paper.

Step 2: Remove the stems from the portobello mushrooms and gently scrape out the gills.

Step 3: In a skillet, cook the ground turkey until browned. Season with salt, pepper, and any desired spices.

Step 4: Add chopped kale to the skillet and cook until wilted.

Step 5: Stuff the portobello mushrooms with the turkey and kale mixture.

Step 6: Place the stuffed mushrooms on the prepared baking sheet.

Step 7: Bake in the preheated oven for 20-25 minutes, or until the mushrooms are tender.

Step 8: Serve hot and enjoy!

Helpful Tips:

BRINTALOS GEORGIOS

1. Preheat oven to 375°F and clean portobello mushrooms before removing stems.

2. Arrange mushroom caps gill-side up on a baking sheet lined with parchment paper.

3. In a skillet, cook ground turkey with garlic, onion, and spices until browned and fully cooked.

4. Add chopped kale to the skillet and cook until wilted.

5. Stir in cooked quinoa or rice and season with salt and pepper to taste.

6. Spoon the turkey and kale mixture into the mushroom caps and top with shredded cheese, if desired.

7. Bake for 20-25 minutes, until mushrooms are tender and cheese is melted.

8. Serve hot and enjoy your delicious stuffed portobello mushrooms!

Cauliflower rice sushi rolls

Ingredients:
- 1 head of cauliflower
- 1 avocado
- 1 cucumber
- 4 sheets of nori seaweed
- 1/4 cup rice vinegar
- 1 tbsp sugar
- Soy sauce, for dipping

Equipment:
1. Chef's knife
2. Cutting board
3. Rolling mat
4. Rice cooker
5. Bamboo sushi mat

Methods:
Step 1: Cut a head of cauliflower and pulse in a food processor until it resembles rice.

Step 2: Microwave the cauliflower rice for 5 minutes to soften it.

Step 3: Spread the cauliflower rice on a baking sheet and let it cool.

Step 4: Mix the cauliflower rice with rice vinegar and sugar.

Step 5: Place a nori sheet on a bamboo sushi mat.

Step 6: Spread a thin layer of cauliflower rice on the nori sheet.

Step 7: Add your favorite sushi fillings, like avocado, cucumber, and cooked shrimp.

Step 8: Roll up the sushi tightly using the bamboo mat.

Step 9: Slice the sushi roll into bite-sized pieces and serve with soy sauce.

Helpful Tips:
1. Use a food processor to quickly and easily rice your cauliflower.

2. Sauté the cauliflower rice in a little bit of olive oil to remove excess moisture and enhance the flavor.

3. Let the cauliflower rice cool completely before rolling it into sushi rolls to prevent them from falling apart.

4. Fill the rolls with your favorite ingredients like avocado, cucumber, and smoked salmon for a delicious and healthy meal.

5. Serve the cauliflower rice sushi rolls with soy sauce, pickled ginger, and wasabi for an authentic sushi experience.

Quinoa and chickpea Buddha bowl

Ingredients:
- 1 cup quinoa
- 1 can chickpeas
- 1 avocado
- 1 cup cherry tomatoes
- 1/4 cup balsamic vinegar

Equipment:
1. Cutting board
2. Knife
3. Mixing bowl
4. Measuring cups
5. Skillet
6. Wooden spoon

Methods:
Step 1: Rinse 1 cup of quinoa in a fine mesh sieve.

Step 2: In a medium saucepan, combine the rinsed quinoa with 2 cups of water.

Step 3: Bring the quinoa to a boil, then reduce heat and simmer, covered, for 15 minutes.

Step 4: In a separate pan, heat 1 tablespoon of olive oil over medium heat.

Step 5: Add 1 can of drained and rinsed chickpeas to the pan and cook until crispy, about 10 minutes.

Step 6: Assemble your Buddha bowl by layering the cooked quinoa, chickpeas, and your favorite vegetables.

Step 7: Top with a drizzle of tahini dressing and enjoy!

Helpful Tips:
1. Rinse quinoa before cooking to remove any bitterness.
2. Cook quinoa in vegetable broth for added flavor.
3. Season chickpeas with your favorite spices before baking for a crunchy texture.

4. Roast a variety of colorful vegetables for added nutrients.

5. Top your Buddha bowl with a creamy tahini dressing or yogurt sauce.

6. Include fresh herbs like cilantro or parsley for added freshness.

7. Add a protein source like grilled chicken or tofu for a complete meal.

8. Don't be afraid to get creative with different ingredient combinations.

Chicken and vegetable curry in a coconut sauce

Ingredients:
- 1 lb chicken breast, cubed
- 2 cups mixed vegetables
- 1 can coconut milk
- 2 tbsp curry paste
- 1 tsp salt
- 1/2 tsp pepper
- 1 tbsp oil

Equipment:
1. Pot
2. Pan
3. Wooden spoon
4. Knife
5. Grater

Methods:
Step 1: In a large pot, heat oil over medium heat and add chopped onions.

Step 2: Cook onions until translucent, then add minced garlic and ginger.

Step 3: Stir in diced chicken breast and cook until browned on all sides.

Step 4: Add diced vegetables such as carrots, bell peppers, and peas.

Step 5: Pour in coconut milk and chicken broth, then sprinkle in curry powder, turmeric, and salt to taste.

Step 6: Bring the mixture to a simmer and cook until the chicken is cooked through and vegetables are tender.

Step 7: Serve over rice and garnish with fresh cilantro. Enjoy your delicious chicken and vegetable curry in a coconut sauce!

Helpful Tips:
1. Start by marinating the chicken pieces with salt, turmeric, and ginger-garlic paste for added flavor.

2. Use a mix of fresh vegetables like bell peppers, carrots, and peas for added texture and nutrition.

3. Toast whole spices like cumin seeds, coriander seeds, and cardamom pods to enhance the aroma of the curry.

4. Use coconut milk for a rich and creamy sauce, adding it towards the end of cooking to prevent curdling.

5. Adjust the spices and seasonings according to your taste preferences, adding a squeeze of lime juice for a touch of freshness.

Baked salmon with asparagus and cherry tomatoes

Ingredients:
- 4 salmon fillets
- 1 bunch of asparagus
- 1 pint of cherry tomatoes
- Salt, pepper, olive oil

Equipment:
1. Baking dish
2. Saute pan
3. Tongs
4. Mixing bowl
5. Sheet pan
6. Chef's knife

Methods:
Step 1: Preheat the oven to 400°F.

Step 2: Place the salmon fillets on a lined baking sheet.

Step 3: Drizzle olive oil over the salmon and season with salt, pepper, and your choice of herbs.

Step 4: Arrange asparagus and cherry tomatoes around the salmon on the baking sheet.

Step 5: Drizzle olive oil over the vegetables and season with salt and pepper.

Step 6: Bake in the preheated oven for 15-20 minutes, or until the salmon is cooked through and vegetables are tender.

Step 7: Serve hot and enjoy your delicious baked salmon with asparagus and cherry tomatoes.

Helpful Tips:
1. Preheat your oven to 400°F and line a baking sheet with parchment paper.

2. Season the salmon with salt, pepper, and your favorite herbs or spices.

3. Place the seasoned salmon on one side of the baking sheet.

4. Toss asparagus and cherry tomatoes with olive oil, salt, and pepper on the other side of the sheet.

5. Bake for 12-15 minutes or until the salmon is cooked through and the vegetables are tender.

6. For added flavor, drizzle the salmon with a squeeze of lemon juice before serving.

7. Enjoy your delicious and healthy meal!

Spaghetti squash with meatballs and marinara sauce

Ingredients:
- 1 medium spaghetti squash
- 1 lb ground beef
- 1/2 cup breadcrumbs
- 1/4 cup grated Parmesan
- 2 cups marinara sauce
- 1/4 cup chopped parsley
- Salt and pepper to taste

Equipment:
1. Pot
2. Skillet
3. Meatballer
4. Spatula
5. Serving spoon

Methods:
Step 1: Preheat the oven to 400°F.

Step 2: Cut the spaghetti squash in half lengthwise, scoop out the seeds and place cut-side down on a baking sheet.

Step 3: Bake squash for 40-45 minutes or until tender.

Step 4: While the squash is baking, prepare the meatballs by mixing ground beef, breadcrumbs, Parmesan cheese, egg, parsley, salt, and pepper in a bowl.

Step 5: Shape the mixture into meatballs and place on a baking sheet.

Step 6: Bake meatballs for 20-25 minutes or until cooked through.

Step 7: Heat marinara sauce in a saucepan.

Step 8: Once the squash is done, use a fork to scrape out the "spaghetti" strands into a bowl.

Step 9: Serve the spaghetti squash topped with meatballs and marinara sauce. Enjoy!

Helpful Tips:

BRINTALOS GEORGIOS

1. Preheat your oven to 400°F.

2. Cut the spaghetti squash in half lengthwise and scoop out the seeds.

3. Drizzle olive oil over both halves and season with salt and pepper.

4. Place the squash cut-side down on a baking sheet and roast for 40-45 minutes or until tender.

5. While the squash is cooking, prepare your favorite meatball recipe and marinara sauce.

6. Heat the marinara sauce in a saucepan.

7. Once the squash is cooked and cooled slightly, use a fork to shred the flesh into "noodles."

8. Serve the spaghetti squash topped with meatballs and marinara sauce. Enjoy!

Chicken and vegetable kebabs with tzatziki sauce

Ingredients:
- 1 lb chicken breast, cubed
- 1 red bell pepper, cut into chunks
- 1 zucchini, sliced
- 1/2 cup cherry tomatoes
- 1/2 cup plain Greek yogurt
- 1/2 cucumber, grated
- 1 clove garlic, minced
- 1 tbsp lemon juice
- Salt and pepper to taste

Equipment:
1. Grill
2. Skewers
3. Mixing bowl
4. Cutting board
5. Knife

Methods:
Step 1: Marinate bite-sized chunks of chicken in a mixture of olive oil, lemon juice, minced garlic, oregano, salt, and pepper for at least 30 minutes.

Step 2: Cut bell peppers, onions, and zucchini into similar-sized pieces as the chicken.

Step 3: Thread the marinated chicken and vegetables onto skewers, alternating between each ingredient.

Step 4: Grill the kebabs over medium heat, turning occasionally, until the chicken is cooked through and the vegetables are slightly charred.

Step 5: While the kebabs are cooking, make the tzatziki sauce by combining Greek yogurt, grated cucumber, minced garlic, lemon juice, and dill.

Step 6: Serve the chicken and vegetable kebabs with the tzatziki sauce on the side. Enjoy!

Helpful Tips:

1. Marinate the chicken in a mixture of olive oil, lemon juice, garlic, oregano, salt, and pepper for at least 30 minutes before skewering.

2. Use wooden or metal skewers to thread alternating pieces of marinated chicken, bell peppers, onions, and zucchini.

3. Preheat the grill to medium-high heat and cook the kebabs for about 10-12 minutes, turning occasionally, until the chicken is cooked through.

4. Combine Greek yogurt, cucumber, garlic, lemon juice, dill, salt, and pepper to make the tzatziki sauce.

5. Serve the chicken and vegetable kebabs hot off the grill with a side of tzatziki sauce for dipping. Enjoy!

Beef and bok choy stir-fry

Ingredients:
- 1 lb beef
- 2 tbsp soy sauce
- 1 tbsp oyster sauce
- 2 cloves garlic
- 1 tsp ginger
- 1 lb bok choy
- 1 tbsp vegetable oil

Equipment:
1. Wok
2. Wooden spatula
3. Chef's knife
4. Cutting board
5. Tongs

Methods:
Step 1: Heat oil in a large skillet or wok over medium-high heat.

Step 2: Add thinly sliced beef and cook until browned, about 3-4 minutes.

Step 3: Add minced garlic and grated ginger, stir for 30 seconds.

Step 4: Add sliced bok choy and cook until slightly wilted, about 2 minutes.

Step 5: In a small bowl, mix together soy sauce, oyster sauce, and sesame oil.

Step 6: Pour sauce over the beef and bok choy, stir to combine.

Step 7: Cook for another 2-3 minutes, until everything is heated through.

Step 8: Serve over rice and enjoy your beef and bok choy stir-fry!

Helpful Tips:
1. Slice your beef thinly against the grain to ensure tenderness.
2. Marinate the beef for at least 30 minutes to enhance the flavor.
3. Use high heat when stir-frying to achieve a nice sear on the beef.
4. Cook the bok choy quickly to retain its crispiness and nutrients.
5. Add aromatics like garlic, ginger, and green onions for extra flavor.
6. Finish with a splash of soy sauce or oyster sauce for a savory umami kick.

7. Serve over steamed rice for a complete and satisfying meal.

Quinoa stuffed tomatoes

Ingredients:

- 4 large tomatoes
- 1 cup cooked quinoa
- 1/2 cup chopped spinach
- 1/4 cup crumbled feta cheese
- Salt and pepper to taste

Equipment:

1. Mixing bowl
2. Knife
3. Cutting board
4. Baking dish
5. Spoon

Methods:

Step 1: Preheat the oven to 375°F.

Step 2: Cut off the tops of medium-sized tomatoes and scoop out the insides.

Step 3: Cook quinoa according to package instructions.

Step 4: In a bowl, mix cooked quinoa with chopped vegetables, herbs, and seasonings.

Step 5: Stuff each hollowed-out tomato with the quinoa mixture.

Step 6: Place stuffed tomatoes in a baking dish.

Step 7: Top each tomato with shredded cheese.

Step 8: Cover the dish with foil and bake for 25-30 minutes.

Step 9: Remove foil and bake for an additional 5-10 minutes, until cheese is melted and tomatoes are tender.

Step 10: Serve and enjoy!

Helpful Tips:

1. Preheat your oven to 375°F.
2. Cook quinoa according to package instructions and set aside.
3. Slice the tops off of the tomatoes and carefully scoop out the insides.

4. Mix cooked quinoa with your choice of vegetables, herbs, and seasonings.

5. Stuff the quinoa mixture into the hollowed-out tomatoes.

6. Place stuffed tomatoes on a baking sheet and bake for 15-20 minutes, or until tomatoes are tender.

7. Optional: top with cheese or breadcrumbs for added flavor.

8. Serve hot as a side dish or main course. Enjoy!

Chicken and vegetable fajitas with lettuce wraps

Ingredients:
- 1 lb chicken breast
- 1 red bell pepper
- 1 yellow bell pepper
- 1 onion
- 1 avocado
- 2 tomatoes
- 1 head of lettuce

Equipment:
1. Skillet
2. Tongs
3. Cutting board
4. Chef's knife
5. Mixing bowl
6. Spatula

Methods:
Step 1: Marinate chicken breast strips in a mixture of lime juice, chili powder, and cumin for at least 30 minutes.

Step 2: Heat a skillet over medium-high heat and cook the marinated chicken until browned and cooked through.

Step 3: Add sliced bell peppers and onions to the skillet and cook until softened.

Step 4: Wash and prepare large lettuce leaves to use as wraps.

Step 5: Spoon the chicken and vegetable mixture onto the lettuce leaves.

Step 6: Top with salsa, avocado, and Greek yogurt.

Step 7: Roll up the lettuce leaves to create fajita wraps.

Step 8: Enjoy your delicious and healthy chicken and vegetable fajitas!

Helpful Tips:

BRINTALOS GEORGIOS

1. Start by marinating your chicken in a mix of lime juice, olive oil, and fajita seasoning for at least 30 minutes before cooking.

2. Slice your vegetables (bell peppers, onions, etc.) thinly and evenly for even cooking.

3. Cook your marinated chicken in a hot skillet until browned and cooked through.

4. Add your sliced vegetables to the skillet and cook until they are slightly softened.

5. Serve your chicken and vegetables in lettuce wraps instead of tortillas for a healthier option.

6. Top with salsa, guacamole, and a squeeze of lime juice for extra flavor.

7. Enjoy your delicious and healthy chicken and vegetable fajita lettuce wraps!

Baked cod with herb butter

Ingredients:
- 4 cod fillets
- 1/4 cup butter
- 2 garlic cloves
- 1/4 cup fresh herbs
- Salt and pepper to taste

Equipment:
1. Baking dish
2. Mixing bowl
3. Basting brush
4. Wooden spoon
5. Oven mitts

Methods:
Step 1: Preheat the oven to 400°F and line a baking dish with parchment paper.

Step 2: Rinse the cod fillets under cold water and pat dry with paper towels.

Step 3: In a small bowl, mix together softened butter, minced garlic, chopped parsley, lemon juice, salt, and pepper to create the herb butter.

Step 4: Spread the herb butter over the cod fillets and place them in the prepared baking dish.

Step 5: Bake the cod in the preheated oven for 15-20 minutes, or until the fish flakes easily with a fork.

Step 6: Serve the baked cod with a side of vegetables or salad. Enjoy!

Helpful Tips:
1. Preheat your oven to 400°F (200°C) and prepare a baking dish with non-stick cooking spray.

2. Season your cod fillets with salt and pepper before placing them in the baking dish.

3. In a small bowl, mix together softened butter, minced garlic, chopped parsley, and lemon juice to make the herb butter.

4. Spread the herb butter evenly over the top of each cod fillet.

5. Bake in the preheated oven for 15-20 minutes, or until the fish is opaque and flakes easily with a fork.

6. Serve your baked cod with herb butter with a side of roasted vegetables or a fresh salad for a complete meal. Enjoy!

Cauliflower cheesy breadsticks

Ingredients:
- 1 medium cauliflower
- 1 cup shredded mozzarella
- 1/4 cup grated parmesan
- 1 tsp garlic powder
- 1/2 tsp salt
- 1/2 tsp pepper
- 2 eggs

Equipment:
1. Mixing bowl
2. Whisk
3. Baking sheet
4. Grater
5. Knife

Methods:
Step 1: Preheat the oven to 425°F and line a baking sheet with parchment paper.

Step 2: Cut cauliflower into florets and steam until tender. Drain and let cool.

Step 3: In a food processor, pulse the cauliflower until it resembles rice.

Step 4: Transfer the cauliflower rice to a clean kitchen towel and squeeze out excess moisture.

Step 5: In a bowl, mix the cauliflower rice with shredded mozzarella, grated Parmesan, eggs, and seasonings.

Step 6: Spread the mixture into a rectangle shape on the prepared baking sheet.

Step 7: Bake for 25-30 minutes, or until golden and firm.

Step 8: Slice into breadsticks and serve with marinara sauce. Enjoy!

Helpful Tips:

1. Preheat your oven to ensure it reaches the proper temperature for baking the breadsticks.

2. Use parchment paper to line your baking sheet to prevent sticking and make cleanup easier.

3. Be sure to squeeze as much moisture as possible out of the cauliflower to avoid a soggy end result.

4. Don't skip steaming or cooking the cauliflower before mashing it into a dough-like consistency.

5. Experiment with different cheeses for varied flavor profiles – cheddar, parmesan, and mozzarella are popular choices.

6. Feel free to add in herbs or spices such as garlic powder or Italian seasoning to enhance the taste.

7. Allow the breadsticks to cool slightly before cutting into strips for easier slicing.

Beef and Brussels sprout stir-fry

Ingredients:
- 1 lb beef sirloin, thinly sliced
- 1 lb Brussels sprouts, halved
- 1/4 cup soy sauce
- 2 cloves garlic, minced

Equipment:
1. Wok
2. Spatula
3. Knife
4. Cutting board
5. Tongs

Methods:
Step 1: Begin by slicing 1 pound of beef thinly against the grain.

Step 2: Heat 2 tablespoons of oil in a large skillet on medium-high heat.

Step 3: Add the sliced beef to the skillet and cook until browned, then remove from the pan.

Step 4: In the same skillet, add 1 pound of halved Brussels sprouts and 1 diced onion.

Step 5: Cook until the Brussels sprouts are tender-crisp.

Step 6: Return the beef to the skillet and stir in 1/4 cup of soy sauce and 1 tablespoon of honey.

Step 7: Cook for an additional 2-3 minutes, until everything is heated through.

Step 8: Serve hot and enjoy your delicious Beef and Brussels sprout stir-fry!

Helpful Tips:
1. Start by marinating thinly sliced beef in a mixture of soy sauce, ginger, and garlic for added flavor.

2. Cook the beef in a hot wok or skillet until browned, then remove and set aside.

BRINTALOS GEORGIOS

3. Add sliced Brussels sprouts to the same pan and cook until slightly charred and crisp-tender.

4. Return the beef to the pan and toss everything together with a sauce made of soy sauce, rice vinegar, and a touch of honey.

5. Serve the stir-fry over steamed rice or noodles for a complete meal. Enjoy!

Shrimp and broccoli stir-fry with garlic sauce

Ingredients:

- 1 pound shrimp
- 2 heads broccoli
- 4 cloves garlic
- 2 tablespoons soy sauce
- 1 tablespoon oyster sauce
- 1 teaspoon cornstarch
- 1/2 teaspoon sesame oil

Equipment:

1. Wok
2. Wooden spoon
3. Tongs
4. Cutting board
5. Knife

Methods:

Step 1: Heat olive oil in a large skillet over medium heat.

Step 2: Add minced garlic and cook for one minute until fragrant.

Step 3: Add shrimp to the skillet and cook until pink.

Step 4: Remove shrimp from skillet and set aside.

Step 5: Add broccoli florets and sliced red bell pepper to the skillet.

Step 6: Cook until vegetables are tender-crisp.

Step 7: In a small bowl, whisk together soy sauce, oyster sauce, and honey.

Step 8: Pour sauce over vegetables in the skillet.

Step 9: Add shrimp back to the skillet and toss to combine.

Step 10: Serve hot over rice or noodles. Enjoy your shrimp and broccoli stir-fry with garlic sauce!

Helpful Tips:

1. Start by marinating the shrimp with soy sauce, garlic, and ginger for extra flavor.

2. Make sure to cook the shrimp quickly over high heat to avoid overcooking and maintain a nice texture.

3. Cut the broccoli into small florets for even cooking and easier eating.

4. Sauté the broccoli in the same pan after cooking the shrimp to soak up all the delicious flavors.

5. Mix together a sauce of soy sauce, oyster sauce, garlic, and honey for a tasty finishing touch.

6. Garnish with sesame seeds or green onions for added visual appeal. Enjoy this simple yet flavorful dish!

Grilled chicken with roasted red pepper sauce

Ingredients:
- 1 lb chicken breasts
- 2 red bell peppers
- 1 garlic clove
- 1/4 cup olive oil
- Salt and pepper to taste
- 1 tbsp balsamic vinegar

Equipment:
1. Grill pan
2. Tongs
3. Saucepan
4. Blender
5. Kitchen knife

Methods:
Step 1: Preheat the grill to medium-high heat.

Step 2: Season chicken breast with salt, pepper, and your favorite herbs or spices.

Step 3: Grill chicken breast for about 6-7 minutes on each side or until fully cooked.

Step 4: Meanwhile, roast red peppers in the oven until charred.

Step 5: Remove the skin and seeds from the roasted red peppers.

Step 6: Blend roasted red peppers with garlic, olive oil, salt, and pepper to make the sauce.

Step 7: Serve grilled chicken with the roasted red pepper sauce drizzled on top.

Step 8: Enjoy your delicious grilled chicken with roasted red pepper sauce!

Helpful Tips:
1. Marinate the chicken in a blend of olive oil, garlic, lemon juice, and herbs for at least 30 minutes before grilling.

2. Preheat your grill to medium-high heat and oil the grates to prevent sticking.

3. Grill the chicken for about 6-8 minutes per side, or until the internal temperature reaches 165°F.

4. Meanwhile, roast red bell peppers under the broiler until charred, then peel off the skin.

5. Blend the roasted peppers with olive oil, garlic, vinegar, and salt to make a savory sauce.

6. Serve the grilled chicken with the roasted red pepper sauce drizzled on top for a flavorful dish.

Beef and Bell pepper stir-fry

Ingredients:
- 1 lb beef strips
- 2 bell peppers
- 1 onion
- 2 cloves garlic
- 1/4 cup soy sauce
- 1 tbsp vegetable oil
- Salt and pepper to taste

Equipment:
1. Wok
2. Spatula
3. Knife
4. Cutting board
5. Cooking pan

Methods:
Step 1: Heat 1 tablespoon of oil in a large skillet over medium-high heat.

Step 2: Add 1 pound of sliced beef and cook until browned, about 5-7 minutes.

Step 3: Remove beef from skillet and set aside.

Step 4: In the same skillet, add another tablespoon of oil and sauté 1 sliced onion and 2 sliced bell peppers until softened, about 5 minutes.

Step 5: Return beef to skillet and stir in a mixture of 1/4 cup soy sauce, 2 tablespoons of hoisin sauce, and 1 teaspoon of ginger.

Step 6: Cook for an additional 2-3 minutes.

Step 7: Serve hot over rice. Enjoy!

Helpful Tips:
1. Use a high-quality cut of beef such as sirloin or flank steak for best results.

2. Cut the beef into thin strips against the grain to ensure tenderness.

3. Marinate the beef in soy sauce, garlic, and ginger for at least 30 minutes to enhance flavor.

4. Cook the beef in a hot skillet or wok to quickly sear and lock in juices.

5. Add sliced bell peppers and other vegetables towards the end of cooking to maintain their crunchiness.

6. Season with a mix of soy sauce, oyster sauce, and sesame oil for a savory finish.

7. Serve hot over steamed rice for a satisfying meal.

Roasted shrimp and vegetable salad

Ingredients:
- 1 lb shrimp
- 1 red bell pepper
- 1 yellow bell pepper
- 1 zucchini
- 1 onion
- 2 tbsp olive oil
- Salt and pepper, to taste
- 1 lemon

Equipment:
1. Cutting board
2. Chef's knife
3. Mixing bowl
4. Baking sheet
5. Tongs

Methods:
Step 1: Preheat the oven to 400°F.

Step 2: Place mixed vegetables (such as bell peppers, zucchini, and cherry tomatoes) on a baking sheet.

Step 3: Drizzle with olive oil and season with salt and pepper.

Step 4: Roast in the oven for 15-20 minutes, or until vegetables are tender.

Step 5: While vegetables are roasting, season shrimp with olive oil, salt, pepper, and any desired herbs or spices.

Step 6: Heat a skillet over medium-high heat and cook shrimp for 2-3 minutes on each side, until pink and opaque.

Step 7: In a large bowl, toss together roasted vegetables, shrimp, and mixed greens.

Step 8: Drizzle with your favorite dressing and serve. Enjoy!

Helpful Tips:
1. Preheat your oven to 400°F to ensure even cooking.

2. Season your shrimp with olive oil, salt, and pepper to enhance flavor.

3. Utilize a large baking sheet or roasting pan to ensure all ingredients cook evenly.

4. Remember to toss your vegetables in olive oil and your desired seasonings for added flavor.

5. Roast the shrimp and vegetables for approximately 15-20 minutes, or until the shrimp is pink and opaque.

6. Allow the dish to cool slightly before assembling your salad to prevent wilting.

7. Serve your roasted shrimp and vegetable salad with a light vinaigrette for a delicious finishing touch.

Turkey and vegetable stuffed bell peppers

Ingredients:
- 4 bell peppers
- 1 lb ground turkey
- 1 cup cooked quinoa
- 1/2 cup diced tomatoes
- 1/4 cup diced onion
- 1/4 cup shredded cheese

Equipment:
1. Knife
2. Cutting board
3. Large skillet
4. Baking dish
5. Mixing bowl
6. Spoon

Methods:
Step 1: Preheat the oven to 375°F.

Step 2: Cut off the tops of the bell peppers and remove the seeds.

Step 3: In a large skillet, cook ground turkey until browned.

Step 4: Add diced onions, garlic, and chopped vegetables of your choice to the skillet with the turkey.

Step 5: Season with salt, pepper, and any other desired herbs and spices.

Step 6: Stuff the bell peppers with the turkey and vegetable mixture.

Step 7: Place the stuffed peppers in a baking dish and cover with foil.

Step 8: Bake in the preheated oven for 25-30 minutes, or until the peppers are tender.

Step 9: Serve and enjoy your delicious turkey and vegetable stuffed bell peppers!

Helpful Tips:
1. Start by prepping the peppers - cut off the tops, remove seeds, and blanch in hot water for 5 minutes.

2. Cook ground turkey with onions, garlic, and your choice of spices until browned.

3. Mix in cooked quinoa or rice, diced tomatoes, and chopped vegetables like zucchini and mushrooms.

4. Stuff the peppers with the turkey and vegetable mixture, sprinkling with cheese if desired.

5. Place stuffed peppers in a baking dish, cover with foil, and bake at 375°F for 25-30 minutes.

6. Remove foil and bake for an additional 10 minutes until peppers are tender.

7. Enjoy your delicious and nutritious stuffed bell peppers!

Baked salmon with lemon and herbs

Ingredients:
- 4 salmon fillets (4 oz each)
- 1 lemon
- Fresh herbs (parsley, dill, thyme)
- Olive oil
- Salt and pepper

Equipment:
1. Baking dish
2. Mixing bowl
3. Whisk
4. Knife
5. Cutting board

Methods:
Step 1: Preheat the oven to 400°F.

Step 2: Place a piece of salmon on a baking sheet lined with parchment paper.

Step 3: Drizzle the salmon with olive oil and sprinkle with salt and pepper.

Step 4: Slice a lemon into thin rounds and place them on top of the salmon.

Step 5: Sprinkle fresh herbs, such as dill or parsley, over the salmon.

Step 6: Cover the salmon with aluminum foil and bake for 15-20 minutes, or until the salmon is cooked through.

Step 7: Remove the foil and broil for an additional 2-3 minutes to brown the top.

Step 8: Serve the baked salmon with lemon wedges and enjoy!

Helpful Tips:
1. Preheat your oven to 375°F.

2. Place the salmon fillets on a lined baking sheet.

3. Season the salmon with salt, pepper, and your choice of herbs (such as dill, parsley, or thyme).

4. Squeeze fresh lemon juice over the salmon.

5. Drizzle a little olive oil on top.

6. Bake the salmon for 12-15 minutes, or until it flakes easily with a fork.

7. Avoid overcooking to keep the salmon moist and tender.

8. Serve with additional lemon wedges and fresh herbs for garnish.

9. Enjoy your flavorful and healthy baked salmon dish!

Spaghetti squash with chicken and pesto

Ingredients:
- 1 medium spaghetti squash
- 1 lb chicken breast
- 1/2 cup pesto sauce
- Salt and pepper to taste

Equipment:
1. Knife
2. Cutting board
3. Skillet
4. Tongs
5. Cooking spoon

Methods:
Step 1: Preheat the oven to 400°F.

Step 2: Cut the spaghetti squash in half lengthwise and scoop out the seeds.

Step 3: Place the squash halves cut-side down on a baking sheet and roast for 40-50 minutes, or until tender.

Step 4: While the squash is cooking, season chicken breasts with salt and pepper and cook in a skillet over medium-high heat until cooked through.

Step 5: Once the squash is done, use a fork to scrape out the flesh into strands.

Step 6: Top the squash with the cooked chicken and pesto.

Step 7: Serve hot and enjoy!

Helpful Tips:
1. Start by preheating the oven to 400°F.

2. Cut the spaghetti squash in half lengthwise and scoop out the seeds.

3. Place the squash halves face down on a baking sheet and bake for about 40-50 minutes, or until tender.

4. While the squash is baking, cook chicken breasts in a skillet with olive oil until fully cooked.

5. Once the squash is done, use a fork to scrape out the strands.

6. Toss the spaghetti squash with cooked chicken and store-bought or homemade pesto.

7. Serve hot and enjoy your healthy and delicious meal!

Chicken and vegetable lettuce wraps with hoisin sauce

Ingredients:

- 1 lb chicken breast
- 2 cups mixed vegetables
- 4 large lettuce leaves
- 1/4 cup hoisin sauce

Equipment:

1. Knife
2. Cutting board
3. Wok or skillet
4. Tongs
5. Mixing bowl
6. Serving plate

Methods:

Step 1: Heat a large skillet over medium-high heat and add 1 tablespoon of oil.

Step 2: Add 1 pound of ground chicken and cook until browned, breaking it apart with a spatula.

Step 3: Stir in 1 diced red bell pepper, 1 diced zucchini, and 1 diced carrot.

Step 4: Cook until the vegetables are tender, about 5-7 minutes.

Step 5: In a small bowl, mix together 1/4 cup hoisin sauce, 2 tablespoons soy sauce, 1 tablespoon rice vinegar, and 1 teaspoon sesame oil.

Step 6: Pour the sauce over the chicken and vegetables and stir until everything is coated.

Step 7: Serve the mixture in lettuce leaves and enjoy your delicious lettuce wraps.

Helpful Tips:

1. Start by marinating the chicken in a mixture of soy sauce, garlic, and ginger for extra flavor.

2. Cook the chicken on medium-high heat until it is browned and cooked through.

3. Use leafy lettuce leaves, such as butter lettuce or romaine, as a wrap for the chicken and vegetables.

4. Sautee your favorite vegetables, such as bell peppers, mushrooms, and water chestnuts, for added crunch and flavor.

5. Drizzle hoisin sauce over the top of the lettuce wraps for a sweet and savory finish.

6. Serve with a side of rice or quinoa for a complete and satisfying meal.

Turkey and kale stuffed sweet potatoes

Ingredients:
- 4 medium sweet potatoes
- 1 lb ground turkey
- 1 bunch kale
- 1 tbsp olive oil
- Salt and pepper, to taste

Equipment:
1. Knife
2. Cutting board
3. Mixing bowl
4. Baking sheet
5. Spoon
6. Skillet

Methods:
Step 1: Preheat the oven to 400°F.

Step 2: Scrub sweet potatoes and pierce with a fork. Bake for 45-50 minutes.

Step 3: While potatoes are baking, cook ground turkey in a skillet until browned.

Step 4: Add chopped kale, garlic, and seasonings to the skillet. Cook until kale is wilted.

Step 5: Cut sweet potatoes in half and scoop out some flesh. Mash with a fork.

Step 6: Fill sweet potato skins with turkey and kale mixture.

Step 7: Top with shredded cheese and bake for an additional 10 minutes.

Step 8: Serve hot and enjoy your turkey and kale stuffed sweet potatoes!

Helpful Tips:
1. Preheat your oven to 400°F before starting to cook.
2. Scrub the sweet potatoes well and prick them with a fork before baking.

3. Cook the sweet potatoes in the oven for about 45-60 minutes until they are fork-tender.

4. In the meantime, prepare the filling by sautéing ground turkey with onions, garlic, and seasonings until cooked through.

5. Add chopped kale to the turkey mixture and cook until wilted.

6. Once the sweet potatoes are cooked, slice them open lengthwise and fluff the insides with a fork.

7. Stuff the sweet potatoes with the turkey and kale mixture, and top with your favorite toppings like cheese, avocado, or salsa.

8. Enjoy your delicious and nutritious stuffed sweet potatoes!

Cauliflower rice with shrimp and vegetables

Ingredients:
- Cauliflower rice (1 head)
- Shrimp (1 pound)
- Bell peppers (2)
- Onion (1)
- Garlic (2 cloves)
- Soy sauce (2 tbsp)
- Olive oil (2 tbsp)

Equipment:
1. Knife
2. Cutting board
3. Skillet
4. Wooden spoon
5. Grater

Methods:
Step 1: Start by chopping one head of cauliflower into florets.

Step 2: Pulse the cauliflower florets in a food processor until they resemble rice.

Step 3: Heat a large skillet over medium heat and add olive oil.

Step 4: Add the cauliflower rice to the skillet and cook for 5-7 minutes, stirring occasionally.

Step 5: In a separate skillet, cook shrimp until pink and cooked through.

Step 6: Add the cooked shrimp to the cauliflower rice.

Step 7: Stir in any vegetables of your choice, such as bell peppers, peas, and carrots.

Step 8: Cook for an additional 2-3 minutes, then serve hot. Enjoy your cauliflower rice with shrimp and vegetables!

Helpful Tips:
1. Start by ricing the cauliflower by pulsing in a food processor until it resembles rice grains.

BRINTALOS GEORGIOS

2. Cook the shrimp separately in a pan with some oil until pink and cooked through.

3. In a separate pan, sauté your favorite vegetables such as bell peppers, onions, and broccoli until tender.

4. Add the cauliflower rice to the pan with the vegetables and stir fry until cooked.

5. Season with your favorite spices such as garlic powder, onion powder, and paprika.

6. Finally, add the cooked shrimp back to the pan and mix everything together.

7. Serve hot and enjoy your healthy and delicious cauliflower rice with shrimp and vegetables!

Beef and broccoli sheet pan dinner

Ingredients:
- 1 lb beef sirloin, thinly sliced
- 4 cups broccoli florets
- 1/3 cup soy sauce
- 1/4 cup honey
- 2 tbsp olive oil
- 2 cloves garlic, minced
- 1 tsp ginger, grated

Equipment:
1. Chef's knife
2. Cutting board
3. Sheet pan
4. Mixing bowl
5. Tongs

Methods:
Step 1: Preheat oven to 400°F.

Step 2: Cut 1 lb of flank steak into thin strips.

Step 3: Toss the steak in a mixture of 2 tbsp soy sauce, 1 tbsp sesame oil, 1 tsp minced garlic, and 1 tsp minced ginger.

Step 4: Place the steak on a lined baking sheet.

Step 5: Cut 2 cups of broccoli into florets and toss them in olive oil, salt, and pepper.

Step 6: Spread the broccoli on the baking sheet with the steak.

Step 7: Bake for 15-20 minutes or until steak is cooked to your desired level of doneness.

Step 8: Serve hot and enjoy!

Helpful Tips:
1. Preheat your oven to 425°F to ensure even cooking.

2. Use a rimmed sheet pan to prevent juices from dripping onto the oven.

3. Marinate the beef in soy sauce, garlic, and ginger for at least 30 minutes for maximum flavor.

4. Cut the beef and broccoli into similar sizes for even cooking.

5. Toss the broccoli in olive oil, salt, and pepper before adding to the pan.

6. Spread the beef and broccoli in a single layer on the sheet pan for proper browning.

7. Cook for 20-25 minutes or until the beef is cooked to your desired doneness.

8. Serve over rice or noodles for a complete meal.

Shrimp and quinoa salad

Ingredients:
- 1 lb shrimp, peeled and deveined
- 1 cup quinoa
- 1 red bell pepper, diced
- 1 cucumber, diced
- 1/4 cup fresh parsley
- 2 tbsp olive oil
- Salt and pepper to taste

Equipment:
1. Cutting board
2. Chef's knife
3. Mixing bowl
4. Whisk
5. Skillet
6. Tongs

Methods:
Step 1: In a pot, bring 1 cup of quinoa and 2 cups of water to a boil. Reduce heat, cover, and simmer for 15 minutes.

Step 2: While the quinoa is cooking, heat a skillet over medium heat. Add 1 tablespoon of olive oil and 1 pound of peeled and deveined shrimp. Cook for 2-3 minutes on each side until pink and opaque.

Step 3: In a large bowl, combine cooked quinoa, shrimp, 1 diced cucumber, 1 diced bell pepper, 1/4 cup of chopped cilantro, and 1/4 cup of feta cheese.

Step 4: In a small bowl, whisk together 3 tablespoons of olive oil, 2 tablespoons of lemon juice, and salt and pepper to taste. Pour over the salad and toss to combine.

Step 5: Serve the shrimp and quinoa salad chilled or at room temperature. Enjoy!

Helpful Tips:

BRINTALOS GEORGIOS

1. Cook quinoa according to package instructions and let it cool before adding to salad.

2. Season shrimp with salt, pepper, and your favorite seasonings before cooking.

3. Cook shrimp in a hot skillet with a little olive oil until pink and cooked through.

4. Mix cooked shrimp, quinoa, chopped vegetables, and a vinaigrette dressing in a large bowl.

5. Add fresh herbs like parsley or cilantro for extra flavor.

6. Serve salad chilled or at room temperature for best taste.

7. Garnish with sliced avocado or toasted nuts for added texture and richness.

Quinoa and black bean stuffed mushrooms

Ingredients:

- 4 portobello mushrooms
- 1 cup cooked quinoa
- 1 can black beans, drained
- 1/2 cup diced tomatoes
- 1/4 cup shredded cheese

(Note: 23 words, 127 characters)

Equipment:

1. Knife
2. Cutting board
3. Saute pan
4. Mixing bowl
5. Baking sheet

Methods:

Step 1: Preheat the oven to 375°F.

Step 2: Cook quinoa according to package instructions.

Step 3: Remove stems from mushrooms and brush caps with olive oil.

Step 4: In a pan, sauté minced garlic and diced onion until translucent.

Step 5: Add black beans, cooked quinoa, diced tomatoes, and seasonings to the pan.

Step 6: Stuff mushroom caps with the quinoa and black bean mixture.

Step 7: Place stuffed mushrooms on a baking sheet and bake for 20 minutes.

Step 8: Top with shredded cheese and broil for 2-3 minutes until melted.

Step 9: Serve hot and enjoy!

Helpful Tips:

1. Start by preheating your oven to 375°F and cleaning the mushrooms.

2. Cook quinoa according to package instructions and set aside.

3. In a separate pan, sauté diced onions, bell peppers, and garlic until soft.

4. Mix the cooked quinoa, black beans, sautéed vegetables, and spices together in a bowl.

5. Stuff the mushroom caps with the quinoa and black bean mixture.

6. Place the stuffed mushrooms on a baking tray and bake for 20 minutes.

7. Serve hot and enjoy as a delicious and nutritious appetizer or side dish.

Chicken and vegetable stir-fry in a ginger soy sauce

Ingredients:
- 1 lb chicken breast, sliced
- 2 cups mixed vegetables
- 1 tbsp ginger, minced
- 3 tbsp soy sauce

Equipment:
1. Wok
2. Wooden spoon
3. Knife
4. Cutting board
5. Tongs

Methods:
Step 1: Heat oil in a large skillet over medium-high heat.

Step 2: Add thinly sliced chicken breast and cook until browned on all sides.

Step 3: Remove chicken from skillet and set aside.

Step 4: In the same skillet, add chopped vegetables such as bell peppers, broccoli, and carrots.

Step 5: Cook vegetables until slightly tender.

Step 6: In a small bowl, mix together soy sauce, minced ginger, garlic, and a pinch of sugar.

Step 7: Add chicken back to the skillet and pour the sauce over the chicken and vegetables.

Step 8: Stir well to combine and cook for an additional 2-3 minutes.

Step 9: Serve hot over rice or noodles. Enjoy your delicious chicken and vegetable stir-fry in ginger soy sauce!

Helpful Tips:
1. Start by marinating your chicken in a mixture of soy sauce, ginger, garlic, and a pinch of sugar for extra flavor.

2. Cut all your vegetables (bell peppers, broccoli, carrots, snap peas) into bite-sized pieces for even cooking.

3. Heat your wok or large skillet over high heat and add a splash of oil before adding the marinated chicken. Stir-fry until cooked through.

4. Remove the chicken from the wok and set aside before adding your vegetables. Cook until slightly tender but still crisp.

5. Return the chicken to the wok and pour in the ginger soy sauce mixture. Cook for another minute before serving over rice or noodles. Enjoy!

Turkey and vegetable quiche

Ingredients:
- 1 ready-made pie crust
- 1 cup cooked turkey, shredded
- 1 cup mixed vegetables, diced
- 4 eggs
- 1 cup milk
- Salt and pepper to taste

Equipment:
1. Mixing bowl
2. Whisk
3. Pie dish
4. Knife
5. Cutting board

Methods:
Step 1: Preheat the oven to 375°F and grease a 9-inch pie dish.

Step 2: In a bowl, whisk together 4 eggs, 1 cup of milk, 1/2 cup of shredded cheddar cheese, and salt and pepper.

Step 3: Pour the egg mixture into the pie dish.

Step 4: Add 1 cup of cooked turkey, 1/2 cup of chopped bell peppers, and 1/2 cup of spinach to the dish.

Step 5: Bake the quiche for 30-35 minutes, or until the eggs are set and the top is golden brown.

Step 6: Let the quiche cool for a few minutes before slicing and serving. Enjoy!

Helpful Tips:
1. Preheat your oven to 375°F before starting the cooking process.

2. Use a store-bought pie crust or make your own for the quiche base.

3. Cook the turkey and vegetables separately before adding them to the quiche to ensure they are fully cooked and flavored.

4. Beat eggs and milk together to create a creamy custard for the quiche filling.

5. Layer the cooked turkey, vegetables, and cheese in the pie crust before pouring the custard mixture over the top.

6. Bake in the preheated oven for 30-35 minutes or until the quiche is set and lightly browned on top.

7. Allow the quiche to cool slightly before slicing and serving. Enjoy!

Grilled swordfish with mango salsa

Ingredients:
- 4 swordfish fillets
- 1 mango, diced
- 1/2 red onion, diced
- 1 jalapeno, diced
- 1/4 cup cilantro, chopped
- 2 tbsp lime juice
- Salt and pepper to taste

Equipment:
1. Grill
2. Knife
3. Cutting board
4. Mixing bowl
5. Tongs

Methods:
Step 1: Preheat the grill to medium-high heat.

Step 2: Season the swordfish steaks with salt, pepper, and olive oil.

Step 3: Place the swordfish steaks on the grill and cook for 4-5 minutes per side, or until the fish is opaque and flakes easily with a fork.

Step 4: While the swordfish is cooking, prepare the mango salsa by combining diced mango, red onion, jalapeno, lime juice, and cilantro in a bowl.

Step 5: Season the salsa with salt and pepper to taste.

Step 6: Serve the grilled swordfish topped with the mango salsa and enjoy.

Helpful Tips:
1. Preheat your grill to medium-high heat.

2. Brush swordfish steaks with olive oil and season with salt, pepper, and a squeeze of fresh lemon juice.

3. Grill swordfish for about 4-5 minutes per side, or until it reaches an internal temperature of 145°F.

4. While the swordfish is cooking, prepare the mango salsa by combining diced mango, red onion, jalapeno, cilantro, lime juice, and a pinch of salt.

5. Serve the grilled swordfish topped with the mango salsa for a fresh and flavorful dish.

6. Pair with a side of grilled vegetables or a quinoa salad for a complete meal. Enjoy!

Roasted chicken with herb butter

Ingredients:
- 1 whole chicken
- 4 tbsp butter
- 2 cloves garlic
- 1 tbsp chopped herbs
- Salt and pepper

Equipment:
1. Baking pan
2. Oven mitts
3. Meat thermometer
4. Basting brush
5. Kitchen twine

Methods:
Step 1: Preheat your oven to 400°F (200°C).

Step 2: Rinse the chicken and pat it dry with paper towels.

Step 3: In a small bowl, mix together butter, minced garlic, chopped herbs (such as rosemary, thyme, and sage), salt, and pepper.

Step 4: Gently lift the skin of the chicken and rub the herb butter mixture underneath the skin.

Step 5: Rub the remaining herb butter mixture over the outside of the chicken.

Step 6: Place the chicken in a roasting pan and roast in the preheated oven for about 1 hour, or until the internal temperature reaches 165°F (74°C).

Step 7: Once cooked, let the chicken rest for 10 minutes before carving and serving. Enjoy your delicious roasted chicken with herb butter!

Helpful Tips:
1. Preheat your oven to 375°F.

2. Mix softened butter with chopped fresh herbs like rosemary, thyme, and sage.

3. Pat the chicken dry with paper towels and season with salt and pepper.

4. Gently loosen the skin of the chicken and rub the herb butter underneath.

5. Place the chicken in a roasting pan and roast for 1.5-2 hours, or until the internal temperature reaches 165°F.

6. Baste the chicken with pan juices every 30 minutes.

7. Let the chicken rest for 10 minutes before carving.

8. Serve with roasted vegetables or a side salad. Enjoy your delicious roasted chicken with herb butter!

Eggplant and zucchini lasagna with ground beef

Ingredients:
- 1 eggplant
- 1 zucchini
- 1 lb ground beef
- 1 cup marinara sauce
- 1 cup ricotta cheese
- 1 cup shredded mozzarella
- 1/4 cup grated parmesan
- 2 cloves garlic
- 1 tsp dried basil
- Salt and pepper to taste

Equipment:
1. Cutting board
2. Knife
3. Mixing bowl
4. Skillet
5. Baking dish

Methods:
Step 1: Preheat the oven to 375°F and grease a baking dish.

Step 2: In a skillet, brown the ground beef with diced onions and garlic.

Step 3: Add diced eggplant and zucchini to the skillet and cook until softened.

Step 4: In a separate bowl, mix together ricotta cheese, Parmesan cheese, and egg.

Step 5: Layer the bottom of the baking dish with a third of the meat and vegetable mixture.

Step 6: Place a layer of lasagna noodles on top of the mixture.

Step 7: Spread a layer of the ricotta cheese mixture on top of the noodles.

Step 8: Repeat the layers until all ingredients are used, ending with a layer of meat and vegetables.

Step 9: Cover with aluminum foil and bake for 30 minutes.

Step 10: Remove the foil and bake for an additional 15 minutes or until the top is bubbly and golden brown.

Step 11: Let the lasagna cool for 10 minutes before serving. Enjoy!

Helpful Tips:

1. Start by thinly slicing the eggplant and zucchini lengthwise to create even layers.

2. Precook the eggplant and zucchini slices in a skillet before assembling the lasagna to remove excess moisture.

3. Brown the ground beef with onions, garlic, and Italian seasonings for a flavorful filling.

4. Layer the cooked vegetables with the meat sauce and plenty of cheese (mozzarella, parmesan) for a delicious lasagna.

5. Bake the lasagna in a preheated oven at 375°F for about 30-40 minutes, until the cheese is bubbly and golden brown.

6. Let the lasagna rest for at least 10 minutes before serving to set and cool slightly for easier slicing. Enjoy!

Spaghetti squash with turkey meat sauce

Ingredients:

- 1 spaghetti squash
- 1 lb ground turkey
- 1 can crushed tomatoes
- 1 onion
- 2 cloves garlic
- 1 tsp olive oil
- Salt and pepper to taste

Equipment:

1. Knife
2. Cutting board
3. Skillet
4. Wooden spoon
5. Grater

Methods:

Step 1: Preheat the oven to 400°F.

Step 2: Cut the spaghetti squash in half lengthwise and scoop out the seeds.

Step 3: Place the squash halves cut side down on a baking sheet and bake for 40-45 minutes, until tender.

Step 4: While the squash is baking, cook ground turkey in a skillet over medium heat until browned.

Step 5: Add chopped onions, garlic, and diced tomatoes to the skillet with the turkey meat.

Step 6: Season with Italian herbs, salt, and pepper to taste.

Step 7: Once the spaghetti squash is cooked, use a fork to scrape out the strands.

Step 8: Serve the spaghetti squash topped with the turkey meat sauce and grated Parmesan cheese. Enjoy!

Helpful Tips:

BRINTALOS GEORGIOS

1. Cut the spaghetti squash in half lengthwise and scoop out the seeds before baking.

2. Drizzle the inside with olive oil and season with salt and pepper before roasting.

3. Brown ground turkey in a skillet with diced onions, garlic, and Italian seasonings for the meat sauce.

4. Add tomato sauce and diced tomatoes to the turkey mixture and simmer until heated through.

5. Use a fork to scrape the cooked spaghetti squash into "noodles."

6. Top the squash noodles with the turkey meat sauce and garnish with parmesan cheese.

7. Serve hot and enjoy a healthy and delicious meal!

Chicken and vegetable fajita bowls

Ingredients:
- 2 chicken breasts, sliced
- 2 bell peppers, sliced
- 1 onion, sliced
- 1 avocado, sliced
- 1 cup rice
- 1 tbsp olive oil
- 1 tsp cumin
- 1 tsp chili powder
- Salt and pepper to taste

Equipment:
1. Skillet
2. Cutting board
3. Knife
4. Mixing bowl
5. Tongs

Methods:
Step 1: Marinate chicken strips in fajita seasoning for at least 30 minutes.

Step 2: Heat a large skillet over medium-high heat and add the marinated chicken.

Step 3: Cook chicken until browned and fully cooked, then transfer to a plate.

Step 4: In the same skillet, add sliced bell peppers and onions.

Step 5: Cook vegetables until tender-crisp.

Step 6: In a separate pot, cook rice according to package instructions.

Step 7: Assemble bowls with rice, chicken, and vegetables.

Step 8: Top with desired toppings such as salsa, avocado, and cheese.

Step 9: Serve hot and enjoy your delicious chicken and vegetable fajita bowls!

Helpful Tips:

BRINTALOS GEORGIOS

1. Marinate the chicken for at least 30 minutes in a blend of lime juice, olive oil, and fajita seasoning for maximum flavor.

2. Cook the chicken in a hot skillet for crispy edges and juicy meat.

3. Use a variety of colorful vegetables like bell peppers, onions, and zucchini for added nutrients and flavor.

4. Don't overcook the vegetables to maintain their crisp texture.

5. Serve over a bed of rice or quinoa for a complete and satisfying meal.

6. Top with avocado, salsa, and a dollop of sour cream for a delicious finishing touch.

Turkey and vegetable stir-fry with sesame ginger sauce

Ingredients:
- 1 lb of turkey breast, sliced thinly
- 2 cups of mixed vegetables (bell peppers, snow peas, carrots)
- 1/4 cup of soy sauce
- 2 tbsp of sesame oil
- 2 cloves of garlic, minced
- 1 tbsp of grated ginger
- 1 tbsp of cornstarch
- 2 tbsp of honey

Equipment:
1. Wok
2. Knife
3. Cutting board
4. Mixing bowl
5. Whisk

Methods:
Step 1: Heat a wok or large skillet over medium-high heat.

Step 2: Add 1 tablespoon of vegetable oil and swirl to coat the pan.

Step 3: Add 1 pound of thinly sliced turkey breast and stir-fry until cooked through.

Step 4: Remove the turkey from the pan and set aside.

Step 5: Add another tablespoon of oil to the pan and stir-fry 1 sliced bell pepper, 1 cup of sliced mushrooms, and 1 cup of sliced snow peas.

Step 6: Return the turkey to the pan.

Step 7: In a small bowl, mix together 1/4 cup of soy sauce, 2 tablespoons of sesame oil, 2 tablespoons of rice vinegar, 1 tablespoon of honey, and 1 teaspoon of grated fresh ginger.

Step 8: Pour the sauce over the stir-fry and cook for 2-3 minutes.

Step 9: Serve the turkey and vegetable stir-fry over cooked rice. Enjoy!

Helpful Tips:

1. Start by marinating your thinly sliced turkey in a mixture of soy sauce, sesame oil, garlic, and ginger for at least 30 minutes.

2. Heat a wok or large skillet over high heat and add a small amount of oil before adding the marinated turkey, stirring frequently until cooked through.

3. Remove the turkey from the wok and add your favorite vegetables such as bell peppers, snap peas, and carrots.

4. In a separate bowl, whisk together soy sauce, rice vinegar, honey, sesame oil, and ginger to create the sauce.

5. Add the cooked turkey back to the wok along with the vegetables and pour the sauce over everything, stirring well to coat.

6. Serve the stir-fry over cooked rice or noodles for a complete meal.

Beef and mushroom stuffed bell peppers

Ingredients:
- 4 bell peppers
- 1 lb ground beef
- 1 cup mushrooms
- 1 onion
- 1 cup shredded cheese
- Spices, salt, pepper

Equipment:
1. Chef's knife
2. Cutting board
3. Skillet
4. Mixing bowl
5. Spoon
6. Oven tray

Methods:
Step 1: Preheat the oven to 375°F.

Step 2: Cut the tops off the bell peppers and remove the seeds and membranes.

Step 3: In a skillet, cook ground beef until browned. Drain excess fat.

Step 4: Add chopped mushrooms, onions, and garlic to the skillet and cook until softened.

Step 5: Stir in cooked rice, diced tomatoes, and seasoning.

Step 6: Fill the bell peppers with the beef and mushroom mixture.

Step 7: Place the stuffed peppers in a baking dish and cover with foil.

Step 8: Bake for 25-30 minutes, then remove the foil and bake for an additional 10 minutes.

Step 9: Serve hot and enjoy!

Helpful Tips:
1. Start by preheating your oven to 375°F.

2. Cook ground beef in a skillet until browned, then add chopped mushrooms and cook until softened.

3. Add cooked rice, tomato sauce, and seasonings to the beef mixture.

4. Cut the tops off of bell peppers and remove seeds and membranes.

5. Stuff each bell pepper with the beef and mushroom mixture.

6. Place stuffed bell peppers in a baking dish and cover with foil.

7. Bake for 25-30 minutes until peppers are tender.

8. Top with shredded cheese and bake for an additional 5 minutes until melted.

9. Serve hot and enjoy your delicious meal!

Quinoa and black bean burrito bowls

Ingredients:
- 1 cup quinoa
- 1 can black beans
- 1 avocado
- 1 bell pepper
- 1 lime
- 1 tsp cumin
- 1 tsp garlic powder
- 1 tsp chili powder

Equipment:
1. Skillet
2. Saucepan
3. Chef's knife
4. Cutting board
5. Mixing bowl

Methods:
Step 1: Cook the quinoa according to package instructions.

Step 2: In a separate pan, heat olive oil over medium heat.

Step 3: Add chopped onion and garlic, sauté until fragrant.

Step 4: Mix in cooked black beans, corn, diced tomatoes, and your favorite seasonings.

Step 5: Let simmer for 5-10 minutes, stirring occasionally.

Step 6: Assemble your burrito bowls by layering quinoa on the bottom.

Step 7: Top with the black bean mixture.

Step 8: Add your favorite toppings such as avocado, salsa, cheese, and cilantro.

Step 9: Enjoy your healthy and delicious quinoa and black bean burrito bowls!

Helpful Tips:
1. Rinse the quinoa before cooking to remove the bitter outer coating.

2. Cook the quinoa in vegetable broth for added flavor.

3. Season the black beans with cumin, paprika, and garlic for a tasty addition.

4. Get creative with toppings like avocado, salsa, cilantro, and lime juice.

5. Don't forget to add some shredded cheese or a dollop of sour cream for a creamy finish.

6. Consider adding roasted vegetables like sweet potatoes or bell peppers for added nutrients and flavor.

7. Mix in some fresh chopped herbs like parsley or green onions for a burst of freshness.

Chicken and broccoli stir-fry with teriyaki sauce

Ingredients:
- 1 lb chicken breast, sliced
- 2 cups broccoli florets
- 1/4 cup teriyaki sauce
- 2 tbsp vegetable oil

Equipment:
1. Wok
2. Spatula
3. Knife
4. Cutting board
5. Mixing bowl

Methods:
Step 1: Cut 1lb of chicken breast into bite-sized pieces.

Step 2: In a large skillet, heat 2 tbsp of oil over medium-high heat.

Step 3: Add the chicken pieces to the skillet and cook until browned and cooked through.

Step 4: Remove the chicken from the skillet and set aside.

Step 5: In the same skillet, add 2 cups of broccoli florets and cook until slightly tender.

Step 6: In a small bowl, mix together 1/4 cup of soy sauce, 2 tbsp of honey, 1 tbsp of rice vinegar, and 1 clove of minced garlic to make the teriyaki sauce.

Step 7: Add the chicken back to the skillet, pour the teriyaki sauce over the chicken and broccoli, and stir to combine.

Step 8: Cook for an additional 2-3 minutes, until the sauce has thickened.

Step 9: Serve the chicken and broccoli stir-fry over rice and enjoy!

Helpful Tips:
1. Start by marinating the chicken in a mixture of soy sauce, garlic, and ginger for at least 30 minutes.

2. Use a hot wok or skillet to quickly cook the chicken until it's no longer pink inside.

3. Remove the chicken from the wok and stir-fry the broccoli until it's just tender-crisp.

4. Add the chicken back to the wok and pour in the teriyaki sauce, letting it simmer and thicken.

5. Serve the stir-fry over steamed rice or noodles for a complete meal.

6. Garnish with sesame seeds or sliced green onions for added flavor and presentation.

Turkey and spinach stuffed acorn squash

Ingredients:

- 2 acorn squash
- 1 lb ground turkey
- 2 cups spinach
- 1 onion
- 2 cloves garlic
- Salt and pepper to taste
- Olive oil

Equipment:

1. Chef's knife
2. Cutting board
3. Mixing bowl
4. Spoon
5. Baking dish

Methods:

Step 1: Preheat the oven to 400°F.

Step 2: Cut an acorn squash in half and scoop out the seeds.

Step 3: Place the squash halves cut side down on a baking sheet and roast for 30 minutes.

Step 4: Meanwhile, cook ground turkey in a skillet until browned.

Step 5: Add in onion, garlic, and spinach and cook until the spinach is wilted.

Step 6: Remove the squash from the oven and flip them over.

Step 7: Fill the squash halves with the turkey and spinach mixture.

Step 8: Top with cheese and bake for an additional 10 minutes.

Step 9: Serve and enjoy!

Helpful Tips:

1. Preheat your oven to 400°F before starting the cooking process.

2. Cut the acorn squash in half and scoop out the seeds and extra pulp.

3. Rub the inside of the squash halves with olive oil and sprinkle with salt and pepper.

4. Bake the squash halves face down on a baking sheet for about 30-40 minutes until they are tender.

5. While the squash is baking, prepare the turkey and spinach filling with your desired seasonings.

6. Once the squash is cooked, stuff with the turkey and spinach mixture and bake for an additional 10-15 minutes.

7. Serve hot and enjoy your delicious and nutritious meal!

Baked halibut with lemon and herbs

Ingredients:
- 4 halibut fillets
- 1 lemon, sliced
- 2 tbsp olive oil
- 1/4 cup fresh herbs
- Salt and pepper to taste

Equipment:
1. Baking dish
2. Knife
3. Cutting board
4. Mixing bowl
5. Spatula

Methods:
Step 1: Preheat the oven to 375°F and line a baking dish with parchment paper.

Step 2: Season the halibut fillets with salt and pepper on both sides.

Step 3: In a small bowl, mix together minced garlic, chopped parsley, thyme, and lemon zest.

Step 4: Place the seasoned halibut fillets in the baking dish and top with the herb mixture.

Step 5: Drizzle olive oil and lemon juice over the fillets.

Step 6: Bake in the preheated oven for 15-20 minutes, or until the fish is cooked through and flakes easily with a fork.

Step 7: Serve hot and enjoy!

Helpful Tips:
1. Preheat your oven to 400°F and line a baking dish with parchment paper.

2. Season the halibut fillets with salt, pepper, and a squeeze of lemon juice.

3. Place the fillets in the baking dish and top them with fresh herbs like parsley, dill, and thyme.

4. Drizzle the halibut with a bit of olive oil before baking for 15-20 minutes, or until the fish flakes easily with a fork.

5. Serve the baked halibut with additional lemon wedges for squeezing over the top before enjoying.

6. Pair with a side of roasted vegetables or a crisp salad for a complete meal.

Cauliflower pizza crust with chicken and vegetables

Ingredients:
-1 small head cauliflower

-2 eggs

-1/2 cup grated parmesan

-1 tsp dried oregano

-1/2 tsp garlic powder

-1 cup cooked chicken

-1/2 cup cherry tomatoes

-1/4 cup bell peppers

Equipment:
1. Baking sheet
2. Skillet
3. Chef's knife
4. Cutting board
5. Mixing bowl

Methods:

Step 1: Preheat your oven to 400°F.

Step 2: Cut a head of cauliflower into florets and pulse in a food processor until it resembles rice.

Step 3: Microwave the cauliflower rice for 5 minutes, then let it cool before squeezing out excess water using a clean kitchen towel.

Step 4: Mix the cauliflower rice with 1 beaten egg, 1 cup shredded cheese, and Italian seasonings to form a dough.

Step 5: Press the dough onto a baking sheet lined with parchment paper to form a pizza crust.

Step 6: Bake the crust for 20 minutes until golden brown.

Step 7: Top the crust with cooked chicken, veggies, and cheese, then bake for an additional 10 minutes. Enjoy your cauliflower pizza crust with chicken and vegetables!

Helpful Tips:

1. Preheat your oven to 400°F and line a baking sheet with parchment paper.

2. Rice or pulse cauliflower in a food processor until it resembles crumbs, then microwave on high for 5 minutes to soften.

3. Squeeze out excess moisture from cauliflower using a kitchen towel or cheesecloth.

4. Mix cauliflower with an egg, shredded cheese, and seasonings to form a dough.

5. Spread dough onto the prepared baking sheet and bake for 20 minutes until firm.

6. Top with cooked chicken, your favorite vegetables, and more cheese before returning to the oven until cheese is melted. Enjoy your delicious cauliflower pizza crust with chicken and vegetables!

Beef and green bean stir-fry

Ingredients:
- 1 lb beef
- 1 lb green beans
- 1 onion
- 2 cloves garlic
- 4 tbsp soy sauce
- 2 tbsp oyster sauce
- 1 tsp ginger
- 2 tbsp vegetable oil

Equipment:
1. Wok
2. Wooden spatula
3. Knife
4. Cutting board
5. Tongs

Methods:
Step 1: Heat some oil in a pan over medium-high heat.

Step 2: Add thinly sliced beef strips and stir-fry until browned.

Step 3: Remove beef from the pan and set aside.

Step 4: In the same pan, add chopped garlic and ginger, stir-fry for about 1 minute.

Step 5: Add green beans and cook until slightly tender.

Step 6: Return the beef to the pan.

Step 7: In a small bowl, mix soy sauce, oyster sauce, and a pinch of sugar.

Step 8: Pour the sauce over the beef and green beans, stir well to coat.

Step 9: Cook for another 2-3 minutes until everything is heated through.

Step 10: Serve hot over rice. Enjoy!

Helpful Tips:
1. Slice your beef thinly against the grain to ensure tenderness.

2. Marinate beef in a mixture of soy sauce, garlic, and ginger for at least 30 minutes.

3. Sear beef in a hot skillet for a nice caramelized crust before adding green beans.

4. Stir-fry green beans until they are crisp-tender to retain their vibrant color and nutrients.

5. Add a splash of broth or water to create a flavorful sauce for the dish.

6. Serve over rice or noodles for a complete and satisfying meal. Enjoy!

Zucchini noodles with turkey meatballs in marinara sauce

Ingredients:

- 4 zucchinis
- 1 lb ground turkey
- 1 can marinara sauce
- 1/2 cup breadcrumbs
- 1 egg
- 2 cloves garlic
- Salt and pepper

Equipment:

1. Chef's knife
2. Cutting board
3. Mixing bowls
4. Skillet
5. Wooden spoon
6. Vegetable peeler

Methods:

Step 1: Heat olive oil in a large skillet over medium heat.

Step 2: Form ground turkey into meatballs and add them to the skillet.

Step 3: Cook meatballs until browned on all sides, then remove from skillet and set aside.

Step 4: Add chopped onions and garlic to the skillet and sauté until softened.

Step 5: Add zucchini noodles and marinara sauce to the skillet, stirring to combine.

Step 6: Return meatballs to the skillet, cover, and let simmer for 10-15 minutes.

Step 7: Serve hot, garnished with grated parmesan cheese and fresh basil. Enjoy your zucchini noodles with turkey meatballs in marinara sauce!

Helpful Tips:

BRINTALOS GEORGIOS

1. Start by spiralizing the zucchini to create noodle-like strands.
2. Season the turkey meatballs with herbs and spices before cooking to add flavor.
3. Brown the meatballs in a skillet before adding them to the marinara sauce to ensure they are fully cooked.
4. Simmer the meatballs in the marinara sauce for at least 10 minutes to allow the flavors to meld together.
5. Toss the zucchini noodles in the marinara sauce just before serving to heat them up without overcooking.
6. Serve hot with a sprinkle of Parmesan cheese on top for an added touch of flavor.

Shrimp stir-fry with broccoli and snow peas

Ingredients:
- 1 pound of shrimp
- 2 cups of broccoli florets
- 1 cup of snow peas
- 4 tablespoons of soy sauce
- 2 cloves of garlic
- 1 tablespoon of sesame oil
- 1 tablespoon of cornstarch
- 1 teaspoon of ginger
- Salt and pepper to taste

Equipment:
1. Wok
2. Stirring spoon
3. Knife
4. Cutting board
5. Tongs

Methods:
Step 1: Heat oil in a large skillet over high heat.

Step 2: Add peeled and deveined shrimp to the skillet and cook for 2-3 minutes until pink.

Step 3: Remove the shrimp from the skillet and set aside.

Step 4: Add chopped broccoli and snow peas to the skillet and cook for 2-3 minutes until slightly tender.

Step 5: Return the shrimp to the skillet and stir in a mixture of soy sauce, garlic, and ginger.

Step 6: Cook for an additional 2-3 minutes until everything is heated through.

Step 7: Serve the shrimp stir-fry over cooked rice and enjoy!

Helpful Tips:

BRINTALOS GEORGIOS

1. Thoroughly pat dry the shrimp before cooking to prevent excess moisture.

2. Preheat your wok or large skillet over high heat to ensure a quick cooking process.

3. Stir-fry the shrimp first until they are pink and cooked through before adding the vegetables.

4. Use a high smoke point oil such as vegetable or peanut oil for stir-frying.

5. Add garlic and ginger to the wok for extra flavor.

6. Work in batches to maintain a high heat in the wok and prevent steaming the ingredients.

7. Season with soy sauce, sesame oil, and a pinch of sugar for a delicious sauce.

8. Toss in the broccoli and snow peas last to ensure they stay crisp.

Grilled steak with roasted sweet potatoes

Ingredients:
- 1 lb sirloin steak
- 2 sweet potatoes
- 2 tbsp olive oil
- Salt and pepper to taste

Equipment:
1. Grill pan
2. Tongs
3. Baking sheet
4. Oven mitts
5. Chef's knife
6. Cutting board

Methods:
Step 1: Preheat grill to high heat.

Step 2: Season steak with salt, pepper, and desired spices.

Step 3: Place sweet potatoes on a baking sheet and drizzle with olive oil, salt, and pepper.

Step 4: Roast sweet potatoes in the oven at 400°F for 30-40 minutes, until tender.

Step 5: Grill steak for 4-5 minutes per side, or until desired doneness.

Step 6: Let steak rest for 5 minutes before slicing.

Step 7: Serve grilled steak with roasted sweet potatoes.

Step 8: Enjoy your delicious and healthy meal!

Helpful Tips:
1. Marinate the steak for at least 30 minutes before grilling to enhance flavor.

2. Preheat the grill to high heat for a perfect sear on the steak.

3. Season the sweet potatoes with herbs and olive oil before roasting for added flavor.

4. Cook the sweet potatoes in a single layer on a baking sheet to ensure even cooking.

5. Let the steak rest for 5-10 minutes before slicing to allow the juices to redistribute.

6. Serve the grilled steak with a dollop of herb butter or a drizzle of balsamic glaze for a gourmet touch.

Milton Keynes UK
Ingram Content Group UK Ltd.
UKHW020738010424
440421UK00014B/883